Spread Your Wings

A guide to five RSPB reserves on the Suffolk coast

Written by Jenny James
Edited and designed by John H. Grant
Project co-ordinated by Colin Coates

Grant-aided by

Local Heritage *initiative*

ISBN No. 0-9514867-1-3

Published by the
Woodbridge Local Group of the Royal Society for the Protection of Birds,
42a Bredfield Road, Woodbridge, Suffolk. IP12 1JE

Printed by
Healeys Printers Ltd Unit 10, The Sterling Complex,
Farthing Road, Ipswich, Suffolk. IP1 5AP

CONTENTS

FRONT COVER PHOTOGRAPH: Marsh harrier, by BILL BASTON
BACK COVER PHOTOGRAPH: Minsmere, by ANDY HAY, rspb-images.com

FOREWORD
by Graham Wynne

The RSPB has had a presence on the Suffolk coast since 1932 when watchers were employed at North Warren to keep an eye on breeding stone-curlews. Land was purchased here in 1939, and then, after the Second World War, came one of the most famous events in ornithological history - the avocet re-colonised the Suffolk coast at Havergate Island and Minsmere. The RSPB swung into action to protect these wonderful, fragile birds and two superb new reserves were born. Outright purchase of these sites came later and their uniqueness was protected. Now, bitterns breed at Minsmere, Dingle and North Warren, while marsh harriers have recovered from just one pair in the UK (at Minsmere) in 1971 to more than 100 nests nationwide in 2004, and avocets have gone from strength to strength.

Our nature reserves on the Suffolk coast now amount to more than 2,000 hectares, stretching from Dingle Marshes in the north to Boyton Marshes in the south. They are home to a huge range of birds with large flocks of wildfowl in the winter, such as white-fronted geese, wigeons and teals, plus thousands of feeding and roosting waders, such as dunlins and lapwings. In spring, the grazing marshes come alive with tumbling lapwings and displaying redshanks, while skylarks are still common. The famous Scrape at Minsmere and the lagoons at Havergate Island host breeding avocets and common terns that can be easily viewed from our many observation hides. In the spring, the heaths come alive with the songs of woodlarks and chattering Dartford warblers; nightingales chorus from the woodland edge. On summer evenings, nightjars can be heard 'churring' across the heath at Minsmere and Aldringham Walks.

Our reserves are not just about birds: they are havens for a huge diversity of wildlife. Otters have re-colonised the waterways at Dingle, Minsmere and North Warren, and water voles can also be found at these sites. Red deer bark out their challenges at Minsmere during their rut on October evenings. On Havergate Island, a thriving population of brown hares has found a safe haven from predators. Butterflies abound on these reserves with good populations of silver-studded blues at both Minsmere and Aldringham, while the scarce grayling and green hairstreak can be found across the heaths. Minsmere and Aldringham also host recently discovered and nationally important populations of the ant-lion, a form of lacewing.

Our Suffolk coast reserves now attract in excess of 100,000 visitors a year. You can visit our flagship reserve at Minsmere, with its visitor centre and wide range of facilities, or stroll around the footpaths of quieter reserves such as North Warren.

I am very pleased to be able to promote this book on our Suffolk coast reserves and congratulate the Woodbridge Local Group on their magnificent achievement. I hope that visitors will find the book a great help in exploring this superb area of the British countryside.

Graham Wynne

GRAHAM WYNNE
RSPB Chief Executive

3

INTRODUCTION

It is a matter of good fortune and privilege to live in this part of Suffolk. Its designation as an Area of Outstanding Natural Beauty is very much a statement of fact.

The area is endowed with an abundant and diverse wildlife, a landscape that gladdens the eye and a rich history. That it retains its beauty and its importance for wildlife, despite the increasing pressures on the countryside, is due to the care and protection tendered by many individuals and organisations, among which we can say without boasting, the RSPB is prominent.

ACKNOWLEDGEMENTS

Producing this book has given us an insight into the skills and dedication of the RSPB's staff, both in offices and on reserves. Our thanks go out to them all but it would be remiss if we did not mention by name the help afforded us by Geoff and Hilary Welch and Andy Needle at Minsmere, Rob Macklin at North Warren, John Partridge and Ian Paradine at Havergate Island, Alan Miller (of the Suffolk Wildlife Trust) at Dingle Marshes and Reg Etheridge at Boyton Marshes.

In total, some 33 people have provided the photographs for this book. Not only are the photographs pleasing in their own right, they are essential to the purposes of the book, which is to show that conservation and habitat management on the reserves provides havens for birds all the year round and enriches the land with a wealth of other wildlife. Each picture is credited and we are indebted to the photographers and organisations for their generosity. Special thanks in this regard must go to the East Anglian Daily Times, the Lowestoft Lounge Lizards wildlife study group, RSPB Images and Mike Page, who provided the aerial photographs.

All the reserves featured are within the Suffolk Coast & Heaths Area of Outstanding Natural Beauty and we are grateful to the Suffolk Coast & Heaths Unit for permission to reproduce the introductory map of the area. The map of Dingle Marshes comes from the Suffolk Wildlife Trust. The RSPB and SWT jointly own this reserve and we appreciate the help of the trust in writing the Dingle Marshes chapter.

Not only have we tried to make this book informative, we wanted it to be attractive and in this regard special thanks must go to the East Anglian Daily Times and its editor, Terry Hunt, for generous provision of facilities in the pre-printing process. Also in the development of the book, Philip Dodd and Richard Widdowson, at our printers, Healeys, have made contributions far beyond those which we had a right to expect.

Before a word was written we had to cover the cost of publishing. We are very grateful to the East of England Tourist Board for a contribution that gave us the encouragement to pursue the quest, culminating in a generous grant from the Local Heritage Initiative. This is a scheme run by the Countryside Agency and funded by the Heritage Lottery Fund and the Nationwide Building Society. The aims of the scheme include the care and appreciation of the local landscape, natural history and culture. These aims we share.

Colin Coates, Woodbridge RSPB Local Group,
June, 2004

North Warren & Aldringham Walks
A lacework of peaceful paths

IN FROM THE NORTH: The grazing marshes at North Warren have become an important wintering site for white-fronted geese, inset

Geography and history

North Warren, between Thorpeness and Aldeburgh, was one of the first RSPB reserves. The wetland heart of the reserve, which has heathland on each side, is the valley of the Hundred River. The mudflats of the original estuary were used in 1912 to create Thorpeness Meare, a shallow boating lake, for the developing Thorpeness holiday village. The lagoons and marshes, shown on 18th century maps as covering the present area of grazing marshes between Thorpeness and Aldeburgh, were also drained at this time.

The land was purchased in 1939, as a result of interest by local naturalists. The original reserve of 37 hectares (90 acres) was part of an area already well known nationally for its interesting breeding birds - among them stone-curlews, bearded tits, Montagu's harriers, garganeys and bitterns. More land has been acquired over the years and the present reserve covers an area of 443 hectares. This includes the heathland of Aldringham Walks to the north of Thorpeness, the area inland from Thorpeness Meare around the Hundred River, consisting of marsh, reedbed and fen, plus an area of mixed woodland and heathland running south to Aldeburgh. Church Farm grazing marshes, east of the old railway line, were purchased in 1990 and the shingle ridge and foreshore from Haven House to Aldeburgh has also been acquired. Much of the reserve is accessible from a network of public footpaths.

Before the Second World War, a system of summer wardens or 'watchers' was introduced. The first was retired policeman Percy Cole, whose 1938 diary records his encounters with trespassers, rabbit-catchers, boys fishing, stray canoeists from the mere and egg collectors. He recorded the annual breeding of Montagu's harriers, then as now a rare and exciting bird.

The reserve has had its difficult times. During the Second World War, the Army built pillboxes and trenches on the heath and wide tank traps across the marshes as part of the coastal defences.

The heathland areas had been kept closely grazed by sheep until the 1930s and after that by rabbits. Following the severe reduction in rabbit numbers from 1953 due to myxomatosis, these heaths became overgrown with bracken and scrub which submerged the heather and grasses. The once-familiar stone-curlew, whinchat and red-backed shrike ceased to breed.

Improved drainage of the marshes had its effect on the wetland areas of mere and reedbeds, where thatching reeds had been harvested until the 1950s. They were drying out and being invaded with willow scrub. As a result, many of the exciting birds for which the reserve had been acquired - such as bitterns, harriers and bearded tits - were no longer in residence.

The presence of the railway line running between Aldeburgh and Thorpeness through the middle of the reserve was not always helpful. Until the line's closure in 1964, sparks from steam engines caused frequent heath and reedbed fires. A particularly damaging one in 1954 destroyed 200 acres of heather.

The present rich and varied appearance of the reserve, with its flourishing habitats and about 86 breeding species, dates from the 1990s. It is the product of years of visionary effort by the warden Rob Macklin, his assistants and a large band of volunteers, many of them from the Woodbridge RSPB group.

Large areas of heather and acid grassland are in good condition, with much invasive scrub removed. These areas support good numbers of nesting nightjars, Dartford warblers and woodlarks as well as a colony of silver-studded blue butterflies. The reedbed has been rescued and the first bitterns since 1946 have successfully recolonised the area. The marshes have been returned to traditional management to attract wintering geese and ducks and breeding and migrant waders.

North Warren is now a very special place, much loved by those who can visit it often and discover its secrets throughout the year.

The reserve is deliberately planned as a quiet retreat, attractive to those who wish to walk the many paths through heathland, marsh and woodland to view the wildlife and birds. It is accessible to all on public footpaths at all times.

ALIVE AGAIN: Improvements to the reserve's reedbed can be seen from the air

HEATHLAND HEAVEN: Aldringham Walks is the heathland home of specialist species such as nightjar, top left, and woodlark, top right

Habitats and management

The reserve is part of the complex of wetland and heathland habitats of the Suffolk Coast & Heaths Area of Outstanding Natural Beauty and is, of course, within the area designated as Suffolk's Heritage Coast. It is part of the Suffolk River Valleys Environmentally Sensitive Area. Its individual quality is demonstrated by its designation as a Site of Special Scientific Interest and parts of the reserve are within a designated Special Protection Area.

The heathland soils are mainly glacial sands and gravels, the marshes are on alluvium and clay, the fens and reedbed on a layer of peat and the reserve is bordered by a shingle beach. Consequently, the reserve contains a diverse mosaic of habitats with areas of reedbed, lowland wet grassland, lowland heath and vegetated shingle ridge. The lowland heath is one of the largest remnants of the once extensive Suffolk Sandlings.

In 1990, the first full-time warden, Rob Macklin, set out to recreate the pristine environments of the pre-war years. His

Photo: CHRIS GOMERSALL, rspb-images.com

THRIVING: Dartford warblers have returned to the Suffolk Sandlings and now thrive on the reserve

extensive knowledge of wildlife, combined with his skills in organising drainage, sluices, mechanical diggers and a host of scrub-clearing volunteers, enabled him to reverse the decline in these valuable wetland and heathland habitats.

In each part of the reserve, management has been targeted at specific species.

Many of the breeding birds of heathland and wetland are ground-nesting and consequently suffer predation problems. Foxes, which can create difficulties on other local RSPB reserves, are not a problem here, however, as there are plenty of rabbits on which they can feed. Regrettably, there has been an apparent increase in predation of woodlark, skylark and nightjar eggs and young by carrion crows and jackdaws. The populations of these corvids have increased hugely in east Suffolk as a result of the rising number of outdoor pig-rearing units being established in the area. The corvids benefit from scavenging around the units for food provided for the pigs but also plunder nests over a wide surrounding area. This is an unfortunate side-effect of this type of humane farming.

Heathland

The vision guiding the heathland management at North Warren and Aldringham Walks has been the restoration of breeding woodlarks and silver-studded blue butterflies. Both flourish

in warm, well-drained locations and low-growing grass and heather. Once widespread, the woodlark declined to only a few pairs on the Suffolk coast by the 1980s and increasing its numbers was a high priority. The introduced silver-studded blues have formed a substantial colony. Nightjars were also targeted, this elusive nocturnal bird preferring woodland margins on the heaths. Dartford warblers have also colonised the area. As this species increased in numbers nationally it was able to spread into the newly revitalised habitats on the Suffolk Sandlings.

The restoration of the acid grass and heather has been a major task, involving the removal of acres of invasive silver birch and pine scrub. Some has been cleared with machinery, but much of it has been taken out by local volunteers on their monthly work parties. The suffocating bracken has had to be tackled by cutting, treatment with a selective herbicide and then removing the deep litter. The heather is flourishing in the north of the reserve and can now be managed by cutting a small area each year on a 20-year rotation to provide a mosaic of vegetation heights. Visitors in the summer can now admire the swathes of purple heather or ling. Gorse is a valuable wildlife habitat - whitethroats, linnets and yellowhammers breed in the thickets and Dartford warblers can be seen singing from the tops of the bushes. However, it needs careful control by coppicing, which is done in a 10-12 year rotation. Rabbits have been a mixed

ACCESS POINT: A footpath sign guides visitors across the marshes from the Aldeburgh-Thorpeness road near the derelict property known as Sluice Cottage

blessing on the reserve. They maintain the short sward of acid grass but need to be excluded with rabbit-proof fencing from the areas of young, newly growing heather. In addition to mowing, the traditional management for grassland is grazing by animals. So now the hardy Hebridean and Beulah sheep, both grazers and browsers of tough vegetation, are kept at North Warren and Aldringham Walks. They are highly efficient at grazing off emergent scrub and keeping the acid grassland sward in perfect shape.

Grazing marshes

The purchase in 1990 of Church Farm Marshes, the 98 hectares of land between the old railway line and the sea, began to reverse the decline of this area. The marshes had been drained and used for relatively intensive grazing, so were too dry for wintering or breeding birds. Traditional management methods returned - and so did the birds. Increasing the water levels in winter by sluice adjustment creates areas of shallow flooding on the grassland which are attractive to wintering and migrating wildfowl and waders. The return of flocks of white-fronted geese and wigeons has been a triumph of habitat management and spectacular for ornithologists braving the elements. Lapwings, teals and dunlins are just some of the birds which take advantage of the undisturbed feeding and roosting sites in these wet meadows. Teals in particular feed extensively on the seeds of saltmarsh rush when these areas are shallow-flooded. Waders with probing beaks search out earthworms and other soil invertebrates in the soft, damp ground.

From late March to November, the water levels are lowered and the grass is kept short for breeding birds such as skylarks and lapwings by a herd of up to 200 sturdy and hardy Continental cross-breed cattle. They are moved from field to field through the summer, following the nesting birds as the young fledge. In some of the higher, drier fields where skylarks nest, the grazing is delayed until August. Some hay may be cut in August and September after the breeding of ground-nesting birds is complete. Rushes and thistles are cut but some vegetation is left longer to provide cover for breeding redshanks. Dykes are cleaned out on a seven to ten year rotation, but important reed cover for breeding warblers is retained. The plentiful supply of slow-moving fresh water provides the ideal conditions for water voles and breeding dragonflies and damselflies.

As a result of these traditional farming techniques, the marshes usually support up to 24 successful breeding pairs of lapwings, 20 pairs of redshanks and the remarkable total of 100 pairs of skylarks.

Reedbed

The area of reedbed in the Hundred River valley survived the excavation of Thorpeness Meare in 1912 and draining of the marshes until the 1950s, when further drainage for agriculture critically lowered the water table. The subsequent drying-out of the reedbed allowed willow and alder scrub to invade and the former rich variety of breeding birds was lost.

In 1992 a major project began to lower the entire area by removing up to 30cm of peat and silt and hundreds of willow trees. This allowed the reeds to rejuvenate and provided an extensive new habitat of wet reedbed. Areas of the reedbed are cut and raked every winter to prevent re-colonisation by willow and alder scrub. The reeds on the nearby fen are cut and burned in rotation in late summer to prevent the accumulation of dead stems and to encourage typical colourful wetland flowering plants such as ragged robin, purple loosestrife and southern marsh orchid.

The efforts of all those involved have been rewarded by an increase in the number of breeding reedbed birds. The return of bearded tits, marsh harriers, water rails and finally - in 2000 - bitterns, has been another success story. An additional welcome return is that of otters, absent since 1976 but now confirmed as residents on the reserve.

Walkers on the reedbed boardwalk may hear the pinging calls of bearded tits or see a marsh harrier quartering over the reeds - and so appreciate the beauty of these restored habitats and the wealth of wildlife they support.

Woodland

Although the reserve is chiefly important for heaths and wetlands, there are over 100 hectares of mixed woodland and scrub which provide a superb habitat for a wide range of songbirds such as nightingales and various warblers, finches and buntings.

Some of the alder and oak woodland around the Hundred River has been left untouched, with dead trees left in place for great spotted woodpeckers to drill for insect larvae in the rotting wood. Other woodland in the north, which includes

END RESULT: Major work carried out to enhance the reedbed has produced excellent results, as this view from the old railway line illustrates

Photo: RICHARD RACKHAM

Scots pine and birch stands, has been managed to attract nightjars to the coniferous woodland margins and woodlarks - which feed on seeds, spiders, beetles and other insects - to the open rides. The alder carr in the wetter parts of the woodland is an important breeding place for the attractive, but increasingly scarce, marsh tit. The alder cones also provide winter food for seed-eating birds. Nest boxes that have attracted 170 pairs each of blue tits and great tits can be observed in many parts of the woodland, only a few feet from the ground for easy monitoring of the eggs and young.

The importance of scrub in woodland clearings and margins cannot be overstated. Untidy in appearance to some, these areas sometimes support over 50 singing male nightingales and their partners. Early morning in early summer is the best time to appreciate them and the other songbirds that flourish here.

Shingle ridge and beach

The shingle ridge is a part of the reserve and has unlimited public access. Management of this fragile and interesting habitat needs to protect the vulnerable and nationally scarce vegetation of specialist plants. In summer, some areas are fenced off to protect the fragile sea pea and ringed plovers take advantage of these areas to breed successfully. Little terns have also bred here in the past but are very vulnerable to disturbance by walkers and, especially, dogs.

Fauna

The mammals most likely to be seen by visitors are rabbits. They can be seen all over the grassland areas, running to their numerous borrows when alerted to danger. They are predated by foxes, but with minimal impact on their numbers. There are also badgers on the reserve. It is estimated that there are at least 50 individuals of the increasingly scarce water vole flourishing in the pools and ditches. They are vulnerable to predation by stoats but there are few, if any, mink to deplete their numbers. They are not under threat from the otters that include these wetlands in their territory.

WOODLAND RESIDENT: Great spotted woodpeckers are often seen in the woods

Red deer, fallow deer and muntjac occur in small numbers and can often be encountered at dawn and dusk. Several other small mammals, such as wood mice, harvest mice, water shrews, common shrews and pygmy shrews are a good source of food for the reserve's wide variety of resident and migrant raptors. A small colony of pipistrelle bats roosts in the north of the reserve and can be seen flying at dusk over Aldringham Walks.

On the light, easily warmed sandy soils of the heaths, adders, slow worms and common lizards can most likely be seen on sunny days. The wetlands provide ideal locations for common frogs and toads, smooth newts and palmate newts - amphibians that need water for egg-laying.

The old railway line is one of the best sites in Suffolk for butterflies. Thirty-five species are listed for the reserve in local records kept since 1900. There is a mixture of woodland species, including the familiar red admiral and peacock, and species more common on the open sandy heath, such as grayling and small copper. In May, green hairstreaks can be seen over the extensive gorse patches in several parts of the heath. In late summer, around the tops of the oak trees, the fluttering flight of the purple hairstreak is unmistakable. The special butterfly of this reserve, however, is the silver-studded blue. This species was introduced to Aldringham Walks in 1998

Photos: DR. DAVID HEALEY

HERE BE DRAGONS: North Warren is home to a wealth of dragonfly and damselfly species, including migrant hawker, mainphoto, ruddy darter, left inset, and blue-tailed damselfly

and has established a successful colony with 317 flying adults counted in 2003.

Although less obvious than the butterflies, 260 species of moth have been recorded on the reserve. They include some rarities such as white-mantled wainscot, ground lackey and marbled clover.

The old railway line is also an exceptional site for dragonflies. Hairy dragonfles are followed by brown hawkers and southern hawkers in high summer as they hatch from nearby pools and ditches. The migrant hawker appears here in substantial numbers. Common darter and ruddy darter dragonflies may be seen from the path across the grazing marshes and, recently, red-veined darters have colonised from the Continent. The blue-tailed damselfly, and also the small red-eyed damselfly which has recently spread here, may be seen over stretches of water.

Crickets and grasshoppers are common all over the reserve, especially on the edges of the grazing marshes. The huge size of the great green bush cricket and the noisy buzz of Röesel's bush cricket are both impressive. Glow worms can still be seen at dusk on the heaths and Britain's biggest colony of ant-lions - a type of lacewing - can be found on south-facing sandy banks on the heath and cliffs at Aldringham Walks. The larval pits in which the ant-lion larvae lurk for their prey can occur in large numbers, with up to 3,000 in some years.

PASTORAL SCENE: Imposing pine tress form an impressive backdrop as cattle graze on the reserve

Main photo: ROB MACKLIN

Flora

Each part of the reserve has a range of characteristic plant species which dominate their area but, among these, smaller numbers of other colourful plants - some rare or unusual - flower through the seasons. Some areas of heath are dominated by ling heather, interspersed with smaller patches of bright purple bell heather. However, much of the heathland vegetation is acid grasses, mainly fescues, interspersed in some places with the tall blue spikes of viper's bugloss. Common ragwort, which also grows freely, is allowed to flower as a source of nectar for a range of insects, especially bees and butterflies. However, it is cut before seeding to prevent it spreading.

In high summer, the numerous butterflies along the old railway line take advantage of the nectar of flowering hemp agrimony. Around the edges of the reeds in the fen, bogbean, ragged robin, yellow marsh iris, southern marsh orchids, meadowsweet and purple loosestrife flower in sequence from late spring to high summer and the yellow flowers of the rare marsh sowthistle rise between the reeds with the heads of the reed mace.

In the maze of drainage ditches through the marshes, greater and lesser spearwort and a rare brackish water crowfoot are among the aquatic plants to be seen. In summer the pink sea pea flowers in extensive patches on the shingle ridge, together with the yellow horned poppy and the increasingly rare sea kale and sand catchfly. Bee orchids and the rare early marsh orchid may sometimes be seen in this area.

Birds season by season

WINTER: DECEMBER, JANUARY, FEBRUARY

The arrival of the wintering wildfowl is the highlight of the birdwatching year for many of North Warren's frequent visitors. The view of the grazing marshes from the sea road car park or from the tracks across the marshes is best in the morning, with the low winter sun behind you – and the east wind on your back. Another good viewpoint is from the old railway line. It is also best when it is high tide on the nearby River Alde as estuarine birds will then fly onto the reserve's fields. The arrival of flocks of up to 500 white-fronted geese and over 3,000 wigeons, together with 2,000 lapwings, 1,000 teals and 1,500 dunlins, can be a spectacular sight. In addition, greylag and Canada geese are readily seen. The reserve's speciality at this time of year,

Photo: ROBERT WINCUP, LOWESTOFT LOUNGE LIZARDS

STIRRING SIGHT: Barn owls can sometimes be seen hunting in daylight on the reserve

however, is the petite tundra bean goose. North Warren has become one of the most reliable sites in East Anglia for this attractive species. Small numbers may often be seen grazing in the wet pastures at the northern end of the grazing marshes, although they can sometimes be lost to view for long periods in the undulations of the land.

Good numbers of gadwalls, mallards, pintails and shovelers will almost certainly be much more obtrusive. Redshanks, black-tailed godwits, curlews and common snipe may be searching the mud for worms and insects.

From the shingle ridge, sea-watchers can scan the waves for part of the Sole Bay flock of up to 4,000 red-throated divers. Among these may be part of the bay's 700-or-so wintering great-crested grebes and passing eiders, scoters, guillemots and razorbills may also be seen. Flocks of up to 80 snow buntings occasionally visit the beach to feed among the patches of sparse shingle vegetation. Recently, an extremely rare ivory gull divided its time between the reserve and Aldeburgh beach, staying for several weeks.

The reedbed is best viewed at this time from Sheepwash Cottage on the old railway line. Up to eight marsh harriers have

roosted in the reedbeds in recent winters. From the paths through the woodland, flocks of siskins, redpolls and goldfinches may be seen feeding in the alders and any remaining hawthorn or holly berries may be exploited by redwings or fieldfares.

The first signs of spring can be detected in February when, on warm sunny days, Dartford warblers may be calling on the heaths and woodlarks may be song-flighting overhead. Skylarks will sing over the grazing marshes as the geese, ducks and waders begin to depart on their long migrations north to their summer breeding grounds. In the reedbed, male bitterns will begin booming to claim their territories and attract the females.

Photo: ANDREW EASTON, LOWESTOFT LOUNGE LIZARDS

REDWING: Flocks may be around the reserve, exploiting any remaining berries

SPRING: MARCH, APRIL, MAY

As the winter migrants depart from the grazing marshes, passage migrants temporarily take their place. Passage waders build up from March, when black-tailed godwits are often the forerunners of species such as whimbrel, greenshank, turnstone and ringed plover.

In April and May the reserve often attracts little egrets and sometimes spoonbills call in. Very occasionally, spring rarities such as bee-eaters and hoopoes cause a pulse of excitement. This is a time of year when observers are well advised to keep their eyes on the skies as the reserve has notched up an impressive array of passage raptors.

On warm, sunny mornings birds of prey often pass over as they head north. Ospreys, common buzzards and red kites can be reliably predicted but rough-legged buzzards, and - later in spring - honey buzzards, black kites, red-footed falcons and Montagu's harriers are more unusual. A recent highlight has been two immature white-tailed sea eagles, talon-grappling over the reserve.

In the woodland and on the heaths summer migrants arrive from April onwards and, together with resident species, begin to establish their breeding territories. The first to arrive are the chiffchaffs. Later, the reserve's strong common whitethroat population builds up and has in recent years topped 450 pairs. Lesser whitethroats are less common, but have still reached about 60 pairs. Blackcaps and garden warblers contribute their songs together with the resident blackbirds, song thrushes and mistle thrushes. Nightingales take advantage of the many patches of bramble and low scrub to build their well-concealed nests. On the heath at Aldringham Walks, nightjars return and males may be heard 'churring' at dusk. The lilting song of woodlarks, given during delightful song-flights over the heath and acid grassland, should easily be distinguished from that of the skylark.

On the grazing marshes, lapwings take up their territories on the well-grazed grassland, driving off their rivals with spectacular dives and distinctive calls. When their nests are established they are always on the look-out for predators. Redshanks choose the rougher pasture, laying their eggs in a shallow scrape protected by tussocky vegetation. Over the higher, drier fields the continuous songs of skylarks fill the air as they prepare to raise their young.

Hobbies will be swooping and feeding on the plentiful supply of dragonflies. Among the reeds, heard perhaps but not often seen, bearded tits, reed warblers, sedge warblers, grasshopper warblers and Cetti's warblers will be nesting and feeding their young. In the early morning, the shrill squeal of the water rails will contribute to the dawn chorus. Little owls, barn owls and tawny owls regularly breed on the reserve with long-eared owls also nesting from time to time.

HEALTHY POPULATIONS: North Warren & Aldringham Walks support impressive numbers of breeding common whitethroats, right, and lesser whitethroats, left

Photo: ROBERT WINCUP, LOWESTOFT LOUNGE LIZARDS

NEIGHBOURING NESTER: Kittiwakes from the nearby Sizewell colony can be seen offshore

On the shingle beach one or two pairs of fearless ringed plovers may be breeding in the safe areas fenced off for plants. They may be joined by little terns but the latter's breeding is rarely successful. Nearby, an interesting use of a man-made structure is the colonisation by kittiwakes of the offshore Sizewell Rigs, where the birds' nests are well protected from land-based predators. The colony has built up to something approaching 200 pairs and individuals can often be seen offshore from the reserve.

SUMMER: JUNE, JULY, AUGUST

As the summer passes, the reserve becomes quieter. The nightingales and then the other songbirds cease their territorial singing and their young fledge from the nests. At this time families of young birds such as linnets and yellowhammers can be seen moving through the yellow flowering gorse on the heaths. In the fen, on still mornings, where the spikes of purple loosestrife punctuate the deepening green of the reed heads, groups of bearded tits call as they search for seeds and insects.

The breeding success of the reserve's bitterns can be assessed during these months. One or two booming males can be heard across the reedbed and during the day females can be glimpsed as they return to the nests carrying food for the young.

Marsh harriers also have returned to the reserve and have raised at least 12 young since 2000. Males and females can be seen over the marshes or quartering and displaying over the reedbed. They may be mobbed by carrion crows and have been observed attacking bitterns and magpies attempting to take young from their nests. By July, juveniles will be out over the reeds, both parents flying with their young and passing food to them in mid-air. On the marshes, the calls and displays of the lapwing and redshank parents distract potential predators from their young as they cower in the lengthening grass and rushes. Warm, still summer evenings are the time to choose for visits to Aldringham Walks to hear and see the nightjars in their favourite territory as they hunt for moths at dusk.

The first autumn migrants appear on the reserve in July and August. These will be breeding birds from as far north as the Arctic following the coast on their route south. In the beach scrub, especially north of Thorpeness, smaller birds such as redstarts and pied flycatchers can be seen resting and the first flocks of curlews arrive

Reserve reflections: special memories of North Warren

Memories of the Monty's, 1955

Stuart Keith was warden of North Warren in 1955 and had the privilege of watching breeding Montagu's harriers on his 'patch'. Perhaps one day the reserve will again host these rare, elegant raptors. We can but hope – until then we can enjoy the spectacle in words. Stuart takes up the tale....

From June 27th I had established the locality in which we might expect to find the female bird sitting. Although the male would roam far afield from time to time, and sometimes for an hour or more, the female rose into the air only occasionally and for very short spells. On the return of the male after one of his roaming flights he always returned to the same spot, which was a fairly large tract of dried reeds quite close to the railway line from Aldeburgh to Thorpeness. Neither bird paid any attention to the passing trains at any time during the summer.

On several occasions I saw the female rise on the return of the male for an aerial pass of food from one to the other. On each occasion she went back to the reedbed.

It was about this period that I definitely established beyond doubt that there were two females and that the male was serving both. The second female was using a nesting site about 150 yards from the other. Although on one occasion I did see the three birds in the air at the same time it was very seldom that both females left the ground together.

There were occasions when the male would take to the upper air and give as fine a display of soaring as I have seen. The bird would drift in wide sweeps, then in circles, rising all the while to a great altitude.

Coming to rest from the air the harriers seldom if ever used the taller trees that grow round the sanctuary, preferring the thorn bushes, dead elders or sallows. More often they favoured an old fence post which would also be used for stripping. I often saw a female visit the stripping post of her mate after he had used it and on most occasions she was able to find some discarded morsel lying at the foot of the post. Whether this was done intentionally by the male I know not, but it happened frequently.

It is difficult to say exactly when the eggs were hatched. It was about the middle of August that I first heard the male calling. The nesting area being approached, he would call very rapidly:-"Chi--ki,ki,ki," and this repeated very frequently. It was a very high-pitched call. It would also be used - rather more slowly - on his return from hunting to bring up the female or, latterly, when there were young, to inform them that he was about to drop some food. The female too used this form of feeding her young and I began to believe the young birds had left the nest and were moving gradually out of the reedbed towards the grassland to the south. During the last days of August I observed four young harriers with a female on the ground with them.

The male at this time flew above with his warning call being repeated with obvious agitation. The young birds soon took to cover in the long, dense grasses. When they were safely hidden the female took wing and both parents flew off to a distance. The young birds looked fit and well. It was not until the end of the month that I saw them on the wing.

to feed on the grazing marshes, with the occasional green sandpiper alongside. The spectacular black-tailed godwits will be in flocks on the marshes from as early as June, their dramatic plumage revealed as they fly up when disturbed.

AUTUMN: SEPTEMBER, OCTOBER, NOVEMBER

The autumn passage continues with redstarts and pied flycatchers passing through, and icterine warblers and barred warblers occasionally

North Warren & Aldringham Walks

Photo: TIM BROWN, LOWESTOFT LOUNGE LIZARDS

ONE TO TWITCH: Although an extreme rarity, Radde's warbler has been recorded on the reserve. Search areas of scrub in October after easterly winds and you may be in luck

being noted, especially in periods of easterly winds in early September. The occasional arrival of a rare autumn passage migrant such as a Radde's warbler or a dusky warbler – again often associated with easterly winds, but later in the season - will attract a great deal of attention.

Out to sea, sooty shearweaters and manx shearwaters may be seen, but more common are gannets and little gulls which sometimes pass in impressive numbers. Skuas can be well represented at this time with arctic, pomarine and great being fairly regular and long-tailed putting in less frequent appearances.

On the grazing meadows, small numbers

of ruff may be seen among other passage wading species such as common sandpiper, greenshank and dunlin. The first groups of wigeons and teals arrive in September, their numbers increasing month by month through the autumn until the huge winter feeding flocks have assembled. As the weather turns colder, more winter visitors arrive and by October the first white-fronted geese can be heard calling as they fly over in straggling lines and descend to make their landfall from northern Russia. By the end of November there may be several thousand wildfowl feeding on the marshes, exploiting the plentiful food supplies in this enriched and restored environment.

Photo: ROBERT WINCUP, LOWESTOFT LOUNGE LIZARDS

BRIEF STOPOVER: Dunlins are among the waders which stop by on the grazing marshes to refuel on their long journey south

BEACH BUNTINGS: On winter's days, snow buntings, above, are sometimes encountered on the beach in front of the livestock corral near Sluice Cottage on the Aldeburgh to Thorpeness road, below. Members of the Woodbirdge RSPB group helped in the corral's construction

RESERVE INFORMATION

Opening times

Access at all times from public footpaths only.

How to get there

Public car parks on the beach road just north of Aldeburgh, in Thorpeness and on the Aldringham-Thorpeness road.

Further information

If you would like more information about North Warren and Aldringham Walks Reserve, please contact The Warden, North Warren Nature Reserve, Tel:01728 452177 email rob.macklin@rspb.org.uk

Facilities

- Three colour-marked trails of 9km, 6.5km and 3km starting at Sluice Cottage, between Aldeburgh and Thorpeness

- information boards at Sheepwash Crossing and Aldeburgh, Thorpeness and North Warren car parks

- public toilets at Thorpeness and Aldeburgh

- refreshments in Thorpeness and Aldeburgh

- disabled access on the beach only.

North Warren & Aldringham Walks
A lacework of peaceful paths

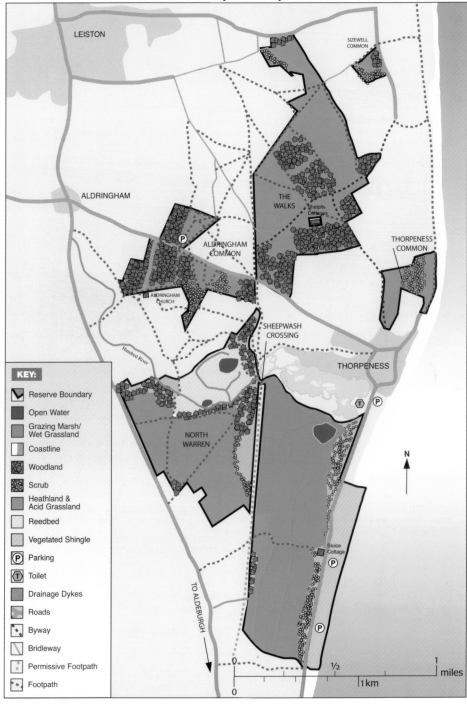

LEISTON

SIZEWELL
COMMON

ALDRINGHAM

THE
WALKS

Shelpits
Cottages

ALDRINGHAM
COMMON

THORPENESS
COMMON

ALDRINGHAM
CHURCH

SHEEPWASH
CROSSING

Hindred River

THORPENESS

NORTH
WARREN

N

Sluice
Cottage

TO ALDEBURGH →

KEY:

Reserve Boundary	
Open Water	
Grazing Marsh/ Wet Grassland	
Coastline	
Woodland	
Scrub	
Heathland & Acid Grassland	
Reedbed	
Vegetated Shingle	
P	Parking
T	Toilet
Drainage Dykes	
Roads	
Byway	
Bridleway	
Permissive Footpath	
Footpath	

0   ½   1 miles
0   1 km

Minsmere
A magical mosaic

A NEW DAY DAWNS: Sunrise at Minsmere. The reserve is justifiably famous for its populations of several species, including bittern, inset

Photo: ANDY HAY, rspb-images.com

Photo: MIKE READ, rspb-images.com

Geography and history

The reedbeds and lagoons of the present Minsmere reserve have had a chequered history. 16th century maps of the area show a broad river valley where the winding Minsmere River opened into an estuary and flowed into the sea at Minsmere Haven.

Natural progression and human intervention gradually changed this estuary into an area of lagoons and reedbeds protected from the sea by a shingle bank and man-made sea walls, the river reaching the sea by means of a sluice. By the 1930s, further drainage had resulted in a patchwork of grazing marshes and reed-filled ditches. These were rich in plant and animal life and supported a wide variety of birds.

At the beginning of the Second World War, in June 1940, flat and strategically vulnerable sections of the East Anglian coast were flooded as a defence against invasion. At Minsmere, the sea sluices were opened and the fresh water exit closed until a brackish mixture of water covered much of the low-lying area of the original estuary.

For five years the reeds spread and flourished in the flooded meadows. By the end of the war, over 150 hectares (360 acres) had been transformed into shallow, brackish and fresh water meres and marsh surrounded by reedbeds. This simple act of flooding had, by chance, created the beginnings of one of Britain's best-loved nature reserves. Plans from before the war were revived, resulting in a leasing agreement between the owner, Captain Stuart Ogilvie, and the RSPB in April 1947. The RSPB finally purchased the reserve in 1977.

The reserve was originally part of the Scott's Hall Estate, which had been developed for shooting. The estate contained mixed woodland with wide rides and coverts around the edges of wet meadows. Gamekeepers controlled predators such as foxes, stoats, rats, magpies and carrion crows. These measures promoted wildlife diversity by

FROM UP ON HIGH: Reedbeds, lagoons, woodland and part of The Levels that help make up the 'mosaic'

providing cover and food resources and by protecting nests and young birds from predation.

In those early days the reserve consisted of 1500 acres (620 hectares) comprising reedbeds and lagoons with higher ground to the north formed by glacial sands and gravels covered by Sandling heath and mixed woodland. The eastern margin was along the sea wall from the coastguard cottages on Dunwich Cliffs in the north to Minsmere Sluice, where the new cut of the Minsmere River enters the sea, about a mile to the south. The southern boundary followed the new cut westward to Eastbridge, about a mile inland.

Recent purchases by the RSPB have added three blocks of farmland on the reserve's northern periphery and an area of grazing marsh, known as The Levels, south of the new cut.

It is here that the evocative ruins of the original Leiston Abbey can be seen. Founded in 1182, it was surrounded by embankments built by monks to keep the sea at bay. In 1363, however, after several years of disastrous floods, the abbey was dismantled. Only the chapel was left, the remains of which are now a much-loved feature of The Levels.

Within its current boundaries, Minsmere embraces an unusual range of habitats. This 'Minsmere mosaic' consists of reedbeds, lagoons, woodland, heathland, wet grassland, acid grassland, farmland and a coastal dune system behind a shingle and sand beach.

The history of the reserve is inextricably linked to the avocet, a species which was lost as a British breeding bird in the mid-19th century. Just as the Minsmere leasing agreement was being signed in 1947 rumours began to spread of the return of the 'awl bird'. Local people had seen four birds on the Minsmere marshes. This was a time when such spectacular birds were at risk from egg collectors and taxidermists, so secrecy was paramount. The birds, code-named 'zebras', were watched over by volunteers. Four nests were found and by early June the first young avocets in Britain for over 100 years had hatched on a muddy islet. Avocets did not breed again at Minsmere until 1963 due to the re-vegetation of open waters and muddy fringes. Fortunately, a successful colony of over 100 pairs built up at nearby Havergate Island.

Since 1947, the reserve has developed and grown, thanks to the devotion of a series of wardens whose love of birds and skill as habitat 'engineers' combined to create today's 969-hectare reserve.

The first part-time warden, Dick Wolfendale, lived in a tent on wages of £1.00 per week. Only eight visitors were permitted each week. The birds and a band of enthusiastic volunteers had the reserve to themselves. In those magical early days, bitterns, bearded tits, redstarts, nightingales, wheatears, red-backed shrikes, nightjars, stone-curlews and many more nested in the rich variety of habitats already on the reserve.

The first hides were made of driftwood, with ex-Army corrugated iron roofs. A pioneering idea in 1948 was the provision of a public hide on the beach side of the sea wall, a revised version of which - a viewing platform - exists today. Driftwood from the tideline was also used to make nestboxes and the first notice boards, gates, bridges and boardwalks on the wet and muddy marsh paths.

In 1959, Bert Axell became the reserve's first full-time warden. By 1962 he had begun to create the first artificial 'Scrape' by bringing in a bulldozer to make shallow lagoons with mud banks and islands to improve feeding and nesting conditions for birds. Bert's innovative management work set the standard which has been maintained through succeeding decades.

The reserve has been at the forefront of the RSPB's research programme on habitat management and restoration, on strategies for halting the decline of threatened species - in particular marsh harriers, bitterns and nightjars – and on breeding waders and predator control.

Over the years, Minsmere has grown with the RSPB. In 1959, there were 624 visitors. By 2003, this had grown to 80,000. Today, Minsmere is one of the RSPB's 'flagship' reserves, showing how people and wildlife can co-exist. There is a core group of full-time, hard-working RSPB staff. They are assisted by volunteers who help at the visitor centre, work at the reception desk, shop and tea-room, and carry out management and survey work. They also help to lead guided walks.

There is a series of visitor trails with hides, accessible by permit, within the reserve and a network of public rights of way around the perimeter. The hides have been renewed and enlarged over the years to improve viewing and to give disabled people access wherever possible. The most recent, Bittern Hide, was completed in 2002 and is built on the edge of the marsh on piles going 20 feet into the ground. Overlooking the reedbed, it affords impressive views of part of The Scrape to the north, Sizewell to the south and Eastbridge to the south-west.

HIDE AND SEEK: The impressive Bittern Hide offers excellent opportunities to watch bitterns

Other visitor facilities have also been greatly improved. The old car park is now a fresh water pond with access for school parties to undertake such activities as pond-dipping. The sand martins can now fly over the water to their nest holes in the sand cliff behind, undisturbed by the traffic. Field teachers run an extensive educational programme for groups of children from schools as far away as London. An RSPB Wildlife Explorers group meets six times a year on the reserve, there are annual Family Fun Days in August and regular Family Activity Days are popular with local families and visitors alike. Explorer backpacks containing a variety of children's activities can be borrowed from the visitor centre.

Habitats and management

Situated on the Suffolk Heritage Coast, Minsmere is part of the Suffolk Coast & Heaths Area of Outstanding Natural Beauty. It is part of the Suffolk River Valleys Environmentally Sensitive Area and holds a Council of Europe Diploma - one of only a handful of sites in the UK to do so.

It is a Site of Special Scientific Interest, a Ramsar Site, a Special Protection Area, a candidate Special Area of Conservation and a Wildlife Heritage Site.

The reserve has been continuously managed since the 1960s to provide the widest possible variety of habitats. As a result, 337 bird species have been recorded on the reserve over the years. Of these, up to 90 breed each year. On any one day, especially in late spring, it is possible for keen birdwatchers to record up to 100 species on the reserve. The key to this fantastic success is a healthy and varied environment.

All of the habitats now on the reserve were there naturally at some stage in history.

However, the living world is in the process of constant change and if habitats were left untended the character of the reserve would alter radically.

Therefore, much of the management is directed towards ensuring the conservation and enhancement of the 'Minsmere mosaic'.

Photo: JOHN KERR/ EAST ANGLIAN DAILY TIMES

FIRST-CLASS FACILITIES: A wide range of goods, including books, clothing, optics and souvenirs, can be purchased at the visitor centre, where permits must be obtained before walking the reserve trails and entering the hides. Also at the centre is a popular restaurant where a wide range of refreshments is available

Photo: KEITH MINDHAM/ EAST ANGLIAN DAILY

PIONEERING CREATION: The famous Scrape - a vision turned into reality by Bert Axell

The Scrape

In natural conditions, the daily sweep of tides and annual flooding renews the nutrients in wetland areas, making these potentially among the most prolific of wild environments. However, sea walls and sluices have interrupted the natural cycle. Therefore it was inevitable that the area which is now The Scrape would begin to dry out and that the wealth of nutrients left by the retreating flood waters after the war would be depleted. By 1959, the pools were drying out and vegetation was increasing. There was also a decline in the amount of fresh-water and brackish-water invertebrates such as minute *Hydrobia* snails, *Corophium* brine shrimps, *Chironomus* midge larvae and water boatmen, on which waders feed.

This necessitated special habitat management, pioneered from those early days by the RSPB and which is now, after 50 years, a highly refined art. The then warden, Bert Axell, understood the underlying geology of clay, peat and silt, and had the vision of creating, just inside the sea wall on a thick layer of clay, a series of shallow brackish lagoons with mud banks and islands. These were supplied with a balance of fresh water from the reedbeds and salt water from the sea by a network of ditches, sluices and bunds. The bunds, or earth banks, have plastic pipes passing through them. Right-angled bends, or elbows, on the upstream end of the pipes - with the openings set at the desired water level – allow different water levels to be maintained in adjacent lagoons. Birds can nest on the islands and feed in the shallow lagoons which are replenished regularly with new water and nutrients.

The Scrape needs intensive annual management, with selective cutting of vegetation to maintain a mix of bare, vegetated and shingle islands to cater for the various preferences of the nesting birds. A rotation is being established with sections left fallow, followed by rotovation to dig in the green vegetation as compost. This provides nutrients for the invertebrates. Water levels are controlled according to the time of year and salinities are managed with fresh water to the west, brackish to the east and sea water to the south to encourage specific invertebrates.

The Scrape now covers an area of 19 hectares. It supports 14% of Britain's breeding avocets and provides a safe resting and feeding place for a very wide variety of spring and autumn passage migrants. It is the model for artificial lagoon design in Britain and abroad.

Photo: CHRIS GOMERSALL, rspb-images.com

AVOCET: At home on The Scrape

HI-HO:
Wardens off to work in the reeds, with nest-boxes designed for bearded tits. Below, a male 'beardie' in his reed habitat

Reedbeds

Minsmere's reedbeds of 179 hectares form the third largest block of this habitat in England. The largest is Westwood Marshes, a few miles to the north at Walberswick.

Typical reedbed species at Minsmere include bittern, marsh harrier, bearded tit, otter, water vole and several rare wainscot moths, including white-mantled wainscot which is found in Britain only in the reeds of the mid-Suffolk coast.

Alarm at the collapse of the British bittern population to only 11 booming males - with just one booming male at Minsmere in 1997

- resulted in research involving fitting young birds with lightweight radio transmitters. Tracking has shown that bitterns prefer the wetter, less dense reedbeds and reedbed margins with several inches of water so they can fish from cover for their preferred food species of rudd, sticklebacks and eels which swim freely between widely spaced reed stems. As the reedbeds were becoming denser and beginning to dry out, it was necessary to cut the reeds and reduce their density with local applications of a specific herbicide. This had limited success and so the bed levels of 50 hectares have been lowered using

DRASTIC ACTION:
It looks drastic but it's highly beneficial to the reedbeds and their wildlife. Dredging has created optimum conditions with just the right amount of open water

HORSE POWER: Grazing by Polish Konik horses helps in reedbed management

BIRD IN THE HAND: Researchers with an 11-day-old bittern chick. Right, an adult bittern

mechanical diggers, thus raising water levels within. Reed margins have been increased, drainage has been improved by clearing ditches and, in the fens, grazing with Polish Konik ponies has been introduced. The bittern population has responded rapidly and strongly, increasing to eight males and up to ten females at Minsmere in 2003, with 43 booming males throughout the UK.

HARDY BREED: Manx Loghtan sheep have been introduced for traditional grazing

Minsmere

Sandling heath and woodland

Minsmere contains an important relic of the Suffolk Sandlings, heathland which originally extended from Lowestoft to Felixstowe. Important heathland species include woodlark, nightjar, Dartford warbler, natterjack toad, silver-studded blue butterfly and the rare predatory insect, ant-lion. The heathland is a mixture of open areas of acid grassland, heather, gorse and bracken with scattered patches of pine, oak and birch trees. There are also larger areas of mixed deciduous and coniferous woodland. Maintenance routinely involves cutting heather and gorse, removing invading scrub, trees, bracken and weeds and rotovating firebreaks. Hardy Manx Loghtan sheep have been introduced for traditional grazing.

A fall in the nightjar population to just six pairs in 1980 prompted clearance of invasive birch, pine and oak saplings on the heath. New glades on the woodland edge were created to enable nightjars to hunt moths along the tree margins. By 1989, nightjar numbers were recovering and in 2003 reached 22 pairs.

A pioneering experiment to restore acid grassland on farmland is under way. In 1989, 192 hectares of arable land were bought from the Ogilvie Estate, of which 158 hectares are being reverted to acid grassland and heath. The first task was to deplete the soil of nutrients. Various methods have been used, such as acidification using sulphur and bracken mulch, continued arable cropping with minimal artificial fertiliser, and continued cutting and clearing of vegetation.

In 2003, the first two fields were ready to be sown with grasses such as bents and fescues for close grazing by sheep and rabbits. In the 20% of the area where heather is planned, mowings from the harvesting of heather seedheads from elsewhere on the reserve will be spread.

NOT AS FIERCE AS THEY LOOK: The Manx Loghtans seem to enjoy taking a break from grazing and tucking in to some alternative nourishment

Photo: COLIN SHAW/ EAST ANGLIAN DAILY TIMES

t is hoped that these measures will encourage recolonisation by stone-curlews, which need low vegetation and patches of bare ground. It should also provide a breeding habitat for woodlarks and, perhaps, wheatears. Part of the farmland will be traditionally farmed and will incorporate low-intensity features, such as winter stubble and spring-sown arable, with acid grassland margins providing food for wintering birds such as larks, finches and buntings. This is an example of traditional farming methods maintaining wildlife diversity.

In the mixed deciduous woodland, coppicing is maintaining the diversity of breeding birds and encouraging nightingales by creating a mixture of dense under-storey and open spaces. New oaks are being planted and old dead trees are left in place to provide feeding and nesting habitat for woodpeckers. Beetles and other insects colonise decaying trees and fallen branches, thereby providing food for woodland birds.

Reserve reflections: special memories of Minsmere

"The Storm"

❛ Waking on Friday, October 16, 1987, the light poured into my bungalow on the Minsmere reserve. Too much light. I looked out of the window and realised I had slept soundly through a terrible storm, one that had felled many of the great oaks surrounding my home. I went into the kitchen. No electric power, a state of affairs that was to last for nearly three weeks.

Outside, the strong smell of crushed leaves hung in the air as I walked with my colleagues, Rob Macklin and Ian Robinson, to inspect the damage. Mature oaks and beech trees blocked the road out of the reserve, but worse was the fate of our magnificent avenue of lime trees lining the road to Eastbridge - nearly 50 trees down in not much more than 100 yards. Very emotional feelings started to well up inside.

Altogether we found we had some 300 mature trees to clear from the two roads leading out of the reserve. Fortunately, I was trained to use a chainsaw and so, with Rob and Ian heading teams of volunteers, we began removing the felled trees. This continued until the Monday morning when Rob and Ian took over the chainsaw work. By then I was nearly crippled with severe aching in my arms due to the sustained use of the chainsaw. In fact, for some years after, I was troubled with both tennis and golfer's elbow in both arms.

Aerial photographs established that over 3,000 trees had come down on the reserve. So was it a disaster? My first reaction was that it was, but in the end it proved to be more of an environmental event. Bird populations were not dramatically changed and flora and fungus species actually increased. In the woods we found many trees had been spared. Today, the scars on the face of our beautiful reserve are healing well. ❜

Jeremy Sorensen, Senior Warden, Minsmere, 1975 - 1991

Minsmere

FAMILIAR SIGHT: Greylag geese and wigeons are often seen rising from the grazing marshes

Grazing marshes

The 138 hectares of wet grassland south of the New Minsmere River are of national importance for wintering wildfowl species, including white-fronted goose, gadwall, teal and shoveler. There is potential for high numbers of breeding lapwings, redshanks and common snipe. The marshes are botanically very rich and also support many species of dragonfly. Management involves control of flood and ditch water levels to create large areas of standing water in winter. In summer, grazing by cattle, hay-making and rush control help to create a patchwork of short swards and rough tussocky grass favoured by waders and other ground-nesting birds.

Foreshore

The plant communities of the 42-hectare foreshore, shingle and dunes give this area European importance. It is one of the top four sites of its kind in Britain. The area is important for recreation so there is inevitable conflict between human access and conservation. Dune restoration projects have included sheep-grazing to reduce scrub and sand sedge. Temporary fencing is used to exclude people from certain areas to encourage the establishment of fragile vegetation. Electric fencing is also erected annually in an attempt to protect a small little tern colony. Despite provision of cover for nests and chicks, this colony has had little breeding success in recent years.

WORTH PROTECTING: Little terns that try to breed on the beach are given assistance

Fauna

As would be expected in such a varied habitat, Minsmere has populations of several small mammals, including water vole - a species threatened in many areas but present here and helped by the reedbed management work. Several species of bat are commonly seen including Daubenton's, which hunts over water, noctule, pipistrelle and brown long-eared. It is likely that many of these breed here. Otters have recently made a comeback and are regularly seen in the reedbed pools. Over 200 red deer flourish on the reserve and in surrounding areas of woodland and heath. The dramatic rutting of the stags can be seen in the autumn. Badgers are well established in at least two locations. Natterjack toad, a rare heathland species, is an interesting introduction. Common frogs and toads breed in profusion in the lagoons alongside smooth and palmate newts. Adders can be seen basking in sunny spots on the heath. Grass snakes, slow worms and common lizards also breed on the reserve.

A wide variety of common butterflies abound in summer and many of these feed on the buddleia bushes next to the reserve centre. Peacocks, red admirals, small tortoiseshells, meadow browns, gatekeepers and migrant painted ladies can be seen on the purple flowering spikes in July and August. Around the reserve, ringlets, Essex skippers, small skippers and large skippers may be seen in the grass along heath edges. Common and holly blues are also present.

Minsmere's heathland is one of the top sites in Suffolk for silver-studded blue butterflies, which feed on bell heather nectar. The larvae feed on the leaves of heather and gorse and, in an intriguing relationship, the pupae are carried by black ants into their underground nesting tunnels from whence they emerge as adults. The rare Queen of Spain fritillary has been seen in several years. In the woodland where honeysuckle climbs up towards the light, white admirals have established an expanding colony. On late summer afternoons, purple hairstreaks and white-letter hairstreaks flutter around the higher foliage of the oak trees.

Several interesting and rare moths breed in the reedbeds, including white-mantled

MIGRANT: The painted lady butterfly can appear on the reserve in large numbers

Photo: ROBERT WILTON, LOWESTOFT LOUNGE LIZARDS

Photo: ANDREW EASTON, LOWESTOFT LOUNGE LIZARDS

Photo: ROBERT WILTON, LOWESTOFT LOUNGE LIZARDS

WINGED WONDERS:
The rare Norfolk hawker dragonfly, above, has been recorded on the reserve. Although its numbers appear to be increasing it is still difficult to see. The white-letter hairstreak butterfly, far left, and brimstone, left, are sometimes encountered

wainscot moth. The wet areas are ideal for damselflies and dragonflies that breed in the lagoons and ditches. The rare Norfolk hawker dragonfly is being recorded in increasing numbers. On warm days in dry, gravelly areas of the dunes, lesser cockroaches - rare coastal insects - may be running and flying around. In the grassland, the loud and varied rasping notes of crickets and grasshoppers fill the air and, as darkness falls, glow worms become visible on the heaths.

Minsmere's other rare and famous insect is the ant-lion, which in Britain is found only on this stretch of the Suffolk coast. Their large-jawed larvae give the species its name. They lie in wait for ants and other insects in pitfall traps dug in the light, sandy soil. Clusters of pitfall traps can be seen on warm, sandy banks on the heathland and near the visitor centre.

UNUSUAL: Glow worms can be seen on summer evenings on the heath, but their larvae, left, are less easily seen, as is such a close-up of a common blue damselfly, above

Although they can be considered as conservation 'tools' the Polish Konik horses and the Manx Loghtan sheep previously mentioned are part of the reserve fauna. The seven Koniks belong to a breed which is a modern recreation of the original European wild horse, known as the Tarpan. They have mouse-coloured coats and a black stripe down their back. They are long-lived and hardy and will graze on rough, wet areas - making them ideal for wetland management. The Manx Loghtan is a primitive breed of sheep and is ideal for conservation grazing on the heathland. They will eat rough vegetation and browse trees. The Minsmere flock was started in 2002 with 30 animals and the lambs born each season now add to its number. It is intended to increase the flock to 50 ewes.

Flora

Single-plant communities dominate on the heath and in the reedbeds. Western gorse and European gorse are found on the reserve and will be in flower throughout the year. In July, patches of the first heather, the bright purple bell heather, are in flower. By August, the full glory of the purple ling, or common heather, turns parts of the open heaths purple and fills the air with its scent and yellow pollen. In the reedbeds *Phragmites* reed covers huge areas, its purple seedheads of late summer turning paler through the autumn and winter.

The wetlands support a wide range of flowering plants. In early summer, the small white flowers of the water crowfoot and the yellow of the lesser spearwort are overshadowed by water plantain and arrowhead. By mid-summer, the purple southern marsh orchid and the yellow iris are found in favoured places in reedbed margins. Later, the locally prolific pink flower of the marsh mallow will be in bloom along the damp edges of the visitor trails and the yellow heads of the rare marsh sow-thistle may be visible among the reeds. The shingle beach and dunes support rare and salt-tolerant plants including the pink sea pea, sea rest-harrow, yellow horned poppy and sea kale. These grow in the shingle, obtaining fresh water from deep below the surface with their extensive root systems. Minsmere is one of the few places in Britain where red-tipped cudweed occurs, producing its inconspicuous flowers in July and August in the sandy fields.

SPLASH OF COLOUR: Salt-tolerant yellow horned poppies are found on the shingle beach

Birds season by season

WINTER: DECEMBER, JANUARY, FEBRUARY

A winter visit to Minsmere for those who can withstand the east coast weather is a most exciting and rewarding experience. The most favourable times are when the wind is from the north or east and when it is coldest on the Continent. The Scrape, reedbeds and grazing marshes are managed so that they are rich sources of food for energy-hungry birds at the coldest times of the year. From December onwards, the reserve is a nationally important haven for wintering wildfowl, with flocks of up to 500 white-fronted geese, 2,200 teals, 350 gadwalls, 200 shovelers and 1,500 wigeons. Many of these will be on the grazing marshes of the Minsmere Levels. Sometimes they will barely be visible in the distance but, when disturbed, clouds of birds will rise up and circle round in swirling flocks before disappearing again as they settle back to their feeding and roosting on the ground. Also wintering on the grazing marshes, though again often well hidden, will be good numbers of wetland species such as common snipe, jack snipe, lapwing and redshank. Small numbers of ruffs and dunlins may also over-winter.

Visitors can see some of these birds more easily, although in smaller numbers, from the hides surrounding The Scrape. Watching birds on The Scrape is one of the highlights of the Minsmere experience at any time of year.

Photo: ANDY HAY, rspb-images.com

Photo: CHRIS GOMERSALL, rspb-images.com

LEVEL BEST: Two species which can be found on The Levels at Minsmere are lapwing, above, and skylark, right

Photo: ROBERT WINCUP/LOWESTOFT LOUNGE LIZARDS

WINTER WANDERERS:
Waxwings are occasionally seen on the reserve

Minsmere

With binoculars or a telescope the birds can be closely observed and their plumage patterns seen in magnificent detail. On a good day, groups of teals, gadwalls, shovelers, wigeons and pintails mingle with waders such as redshanks, ruffs, dunlins, lapwings and curlews. Kingfishers dive from vantage points by the ditches and water rails frequent the reedbeds, though they will often be more easily heard than seen. Also wintering here is a small but highly significant number of water pipits. They can sometimes be seen on The Scrape but more usually frequent The Levels.

To see some of the wildfowl species wintering on the reserve it is best to look over the reedbeds and lagoons from Island Mere or Bittern hides. Here, small numbers of whooper and Bewick's swans, together with tufted ducks, goldeneyes and pochards, brighten the winter days. A search of the duck flocks may be rewarded with the discovery of a scarcer species, such as ferruginous duck, smew or green-winged teal.

Passerine winter visitors can often be seen on the marshes or in the woodland. Bramblings, siskins, redwings and fieldfares visit in varying numbers. With northerly or easterly winds there may also be scarcer visitors around the reserve, such as firecrests and waxwings in the wood and scrub areas and shorelarks and snow buntings in the dunes or on the beach.

Many of the birds for which Minsmere is justly famous can be seen at all seasons, although there can be some winter dispersal to other wetlands in Britain or further south. Marsh harriers can be seen over the marshes throughout the winter. These are predominantly females. Some of Minsmere's young marsh harriers leave the British winter behind and spend time in Spain or, occasionally, north-west Africa. Bearded tits also range widely during the winter but pairs or groups are usually to be seen in the reserve reedbeds. On still, bright winter days their 'pinging' calls attract attention as they feed on seeds in the tops of the pale winter reeds.

Bitterns will be feeding in the reedbed margins, well camouflaged and only occasionally seen at this time. However, by early February their haunting, foghorn-like booming can be heard across the marshes. In the early mornings, the resident water rails, often only located by their squealing calls, search covertly in the pool margins for their staple diet of sticklebacks.

Other hunters are more obvious. Besides marsh harriers, raptors such as barn owls and short-eared owls regularly hunt on the reserve as do hen harriers, merlins and peregrines.

Minsmere

Sea-watching can be very rewarding at this time of year as there are many visiting species from cold, northern waters. The best vantage points are Dunwich Cliffs and the dunes near Minsmere Sluice. Sole Bay holds Britain's largest group of wintering red-throated divers - up to 4,000 birds - and at times hundreds can be seen flying fast and low over the waves. They will be taking advantage of the relatively mild conditions and easy feeding - following the sprat shoals in the shallow water over Sizewell Banks. Among the divers will be great crested grebes, which have a winter population here of up to 700.

Other species which can be relied upon offshore include common scoter, guillemot and kittiwake. Scarcer species which can be seen, given luck, include pomarine skua, little gull and velvet scoter.

The first sign of spring may be a booming bittern or the distinctive sound of an over-wintering chiffchaff on a warm day in early February. On sunnier mornings, woodlarks begin their territorial singing and, high above the reeds, a male marsh harrier may be circling, diving, tumbling and looping-the-loop in the first of his spectacular displays of sky-dancing intended to establish his territory and attract females.

Photo: DAVID KINDRED/ EAST ANGLIAN DAILY TIMES

WINTER'S DAY: A scan of the sea from the dunes can often be rewarded with views of red-throated divers, although this species is rarely seen in summer plumage as shown below. Great crested grebe, inset, is another species often seen

Photo: and inset: CHRIS COMERSALL, rspb-images.com

SPRING: MARCH, APRIL, MAY

By March, the number of wintering birds will be diminishing as they start to move north to their breeding grounds. The number of passage migrants increases throughout the month. Passage raptors can include red kites, merlins, common buzzards and peregrines. Ring ouzels, wheatears and black redstarts also pass through on their way north and common cranes will occasionally be diverted here from their usual migratory route through eastern Europe.

On The Scrape in April and May, among the noisy black-headed gulls and the diving common terns which are jostling for nesting territory, curlew sandpipers, knots, turnstones, grey plovers, black-tailed godwits and bar-tailed godwits may rest and feed before moving on. Ruffs, with the beginnings of their striking summer plumage, may practice their courtship 'lek' before departing.

Other migrants sometimes seen on the reserve at this time include pied flycatchers and whinchats. Overhead an osprey may be soaring, perhaps lingering long enough to plunge into one of the meres to catch a fish. Some vagrants may stay for a few days and, not surprisingly, these attract much attention. Recent spring highlights have included alpine accentor, great white egret, short-toed lark, alpine swift, red-rumped swallow, black kite, white stork, bee-eater and woodchat shrike.

During April and May the reserve is traditionally at its best and the return of the summer migrants reaches its peak.

Photo: JON BURRELL, LOWESTOFT LOUNGE LIZARDS

EARLY BIRD: Black redstart, one of the earliest migrant species to be seen on the reserve

Sand martin numbers build up and they begin to investigate the sandy cliff near the reserve centre.

Many of the woodland birds should be around by now and can be detected by their songs. Blackcaps, garden warblers, willow warblers and chiffchaffs will be singing among the trees with whitethroats, lesser whitethroats, nightingales and turtle doves singing along the hedgerows and in areas of scrub.

Resident woodland birds which will by now have established territories and nests include marsh tits, coal tits, nuthatches, treecreepers, goldcrests, long-tailed tits and sparrowhawks. Dartford warblers, stonechats, linnets, yellowhammers and tree pipits will be singing on the heaths and can be seen from the network of public footpaths and bridleways.

Photo: ROBERT WILTON/ LOWESTOFT LOUNGE LIZARDS

HEAD-ON: Turnstones can be seen on passage, on The Scrape, the beach or Minsmere Sluice when its weed-covered concrete is exposed by the tide

WELCOME INVADER: Cetti's warblers have colonised from southern Europe in recent years

Minsmere has contributed to the dramatic spread of Cetti's warblers into south-east Britain. The thick, low scrub of willow and hawthorn at reedbed margins provides the cover near deeper water which this species needs for nesting and feeding. These secretive birds are best detected by their explosive song of clear, penetrating notes that stops as abruptly as it begins.

Across the marsh, male marsh harriers can be seen bringing in nesting material, flying in low over the reedbeds carrying vegetation in their talons. At Minsmere, each male regularly has more than one female, and each female has her own nest. In most years the reserve supports between six and eight nests. In 2003 a record 28 young were reared.

In the reedbeds, where the green stems of this year's reeds will be growing upwards through the dry winter leaf litter, reed buntings will be establishing their territories and the strident tones of sedge warblers may compete with the 'reeling' of grasshopper warblers. Bearded tits may be taking advantage of the 'wigwam'

nestboxes provided for them, or building their own roofed nests low in the more dense areas. The shy reed warblers will be building their tightly woven, cup-shaped nests carefully bound to the reed stems, always under threat from the parasitic cuckoos arriving from late April onwards.

The late-arriving swifts, with their attendant predators, the hobbies, in full pursuit, can be seen sweeping over the reeds and flying high after insects. The season's influx is completed by the arrival of nightjars announcing their presence with long, churring calls in the late evenings on the heaths.

SUMMER: JUNE, JULY, AUGUST

As summer begins, the breeding season is well under way and the carefully managed habitats are being exploited by nesting birds.

On The Scrape, water levels will be gradually lowered and by June the first fledgling gulls and terns will appear on the mud and islands, surrounded by hundreds of diving, screaming adults. The first downy brown and grey avocet chicks may be foraging along the edge of The Scrape, predatory gulls being kept at bay by the aggressive parents. Brown-downed redshank chicks also explore for food on the wet mud, their parents attracting attention by their anxious, chipping calls. These young birds are extremely vulnerable not only to predatory gulls but also to stoats, weasels and foxes, which may evade The Scrape's protective electric fencing. Sparrowhawks threaten birds of all ages; a sudden clamour and instant flight of hundreds of birds rising simultaneously into the air signalling an attack.

By June and July, parties of mallards, gadwalls and shovelers may be seen criss-crossing the pools, the chicks being supervised by the females. The males stay separate in large groups and moult at this time. From Bittern and Island Mere hides good opportunities arise for the patient observer. Coots, moorhens, little grebes, mute swans and Canada geese can be seen across the pools in large numbers. Grey herons fish along the reed edges and the shrill screams of water rails may be heard. Sometimes a pair of otters may break the surface or a swooping hobby may fly across in pursuit of a swift, sand martin or flying insect, such as a bee or a dragonfly.

Male and female marsh harriers will commonly be seen quartering the marshes, low over the reeds, or perching in one of the small trees dotted around the old field margins of the original farmland. During incubation, hunting is done by the males with the females progressively taking over once the young have hatched. From the hides there are frequent opportunities to watch the harriers' spectacular food passes in which the male passes food in mid-air to the female. Groups of bearded tits may be heard calling and, on still days, they may be seen searching the reeds for insects with which to feed their young. This is the best time to look for bitterns as they fly over the reeds and open water between their nests and their feeding sites. They may also be seen searching for fish, stalking slowly and carefully through the water between the reeds.

Along the scrub-lined edges of the reedbeds, the reeling song of grasshopper warblers may still be heard. On the paths leading to the hides, the purple spikes of the southern marsh orchids flower abundantly, as do yellow irises.

By late June, the woodland areas have become quieter as first the nightingales, then the warblers, complete their breeding and depart.

READY TO GO: By late June, nightingales are among the species which prepare to depart

Photo: ANDY HAY, rspb-images.com

POPULAR BIRD: Wader-watchers are always pleased to see the elegant wood sandpiper

n early July, in what is perhaps the climax of the Minsmere breeding season, the year's young marsh harriers make their first appearance above the reed tops.

Even at the height of the breeding season on the Suffolk coast, birds from further north begin to appear on their way south. As early as mid-June, groups of female spotted redshanks, still in dark summer plumage, will have gathered on The Scrape, having stayed in their northern haunts just long enough to lay their eggs. Other migrant wader species will include lapwing, curlew, dunlin, knot, wood sandpiper and common sandpiper. Among the lesser black-backed gulls which settle on The Scrape may be the occasional Mediterranean gull or small numbers of yellow-legged gulls.

July and August is a busy time for the wader-watcher. Around this period as many as 29 species have been recorded. Most numerous will be dunlins and with them there may be common snipe, green, wood, common and curlew sandpipers, greenshanks, little stints, turnstones, bar-tailed godwits, black-tailed godwits,

golden plovers and grey plovers. Many will still be in their striking summer plumage. Globe-trotting vagrants sometimes appear from far off lands, such as Arctic Canada or Siberia.

ittle egret numbers peak at this time and it is also a good time for spoonbills. The Scrape is quieter by mid-August as the avocets and gulls move to other feeding grounds and the terns begin their migrations, but the duck numbers are building up with the arrival of teals, wigeons and pintails.

IDENTIFICATION CHALLENGE: Sharp-eyed observers may pick out a juvenile Mediterranean gull on The Scrape

At this time, on cloudy nights with easterly winds, many nocturnal migrants which navigate by the stars may become disoriented and make landfall on this coast. By morning, the bushes between the dunes and the sea wall can contain many sedge warblers, willow warblers, pied and spotted flycatchers, lesser whitethroats, redstarts and other small birds, with wheatears, whinchats and meadow pipits on open ground. Fortunate birdwatchers may find the occasional vagrant and drift migrant species such as icterine warbler, barred warbler or red-backed shrike.

Offshore, sea-watching becomes more productive. Fulmars, arctic skuas, common scoters, gannets and little gulls are all regularly seen and the potential for such exciting species as sooty shearwater and long-tailed skua increases, especially in periods of strong, onshore winds.

Photos: ROBERT WINCUP/ LOWESTOFT LOUNGE LIZARDS

ALL AT SEA: Sea-watching becomes more productive in August and species such as fulmar, above, and little gull, inset, can be seen offshore

AUTUMN: SEPTEMBER, OCTOBER, NOVEMBER

This is the season when millions of birds move south throughout Europe from their summer breeding grounds. Many have left areas well inside the Arctic Circle, where in June, July and August there is plentiful food and unbroken daylight in which to find it. But as the short northern summer comes to an end, it is time to head south.

Many birds migrate south-east across the Continent and only arrive on the Suffolk coast if blown off course by easterly winds, giving observers on this coast a chance to see some rare and unusual birds.

At times, in the correct weather conditions, a 'fall' of migrants may occur. Indeed, Britain's biggest recorded deluge of birds took place here on September 3, 1965, when a deep depression over Europe caused a 'fall' of some 400,000 disorientated and exhausted birds to arrive on a small stretch of the Suffolk coast. From Lowestoft south to Minsmere huge numbers of Scandinavian migrants were grounded by a combination of torrential rain and onshore winds. On the reserve, a total of 200,000 small birds of 52 species arrived overnight and throughout the morning. They included wheatears, redstarts, garden warblers, pied flycatchers, bluethroats, wrynecks, icterine warblers, red-backed shrikes and ortolan buntings.

IN OFF THE SEA: Bramblings are among the species which pour in from Scandinavia

Photo: CHRIS GOMERSALL, rspb-images.com

Such a 'fall' is unlikely to be witnessed again but visible migration can still be an awe-inspiring spectacle. Often, around sunrise, flocks of small birds may be heard calling as they pass through - wagtails, bramblings, chaffinches, siskins, redpolls, goldfinches, greenfinches, linnets and huge flocks of up to 50,000 starlings.

The offshore movement of ducks, geese and seabirds continues. Diligent observers sometimes pick out Arctic and black terns on the move and the first big numbers of brent geese may be logged.

By October and November, fieldfares and redwings will have arrived from Scandinavia, accompanied by Continental blackbirds, song thrushes, bramblings and goldcrests. These will be seen throughout the winter months but Asiatic species such as Pallas's warbler and yellow-browed warbler, which can set the pulses racing at this time, are more transient. An impressive array of vagrants has been recorded on the reserve at this time of year, among them Britain's first Siberian blue robin. If that can turn up it could be said that almost anything can.

Wildfowl numbers increase on the meres, grazing marshes and The Scrape. Large flocks of wigeons and teals can be seen and the first white-fronted geese, Bewick's swans and whooper swans arrive, often in family groups, to settle in for the winter.

Photo: TIM BROWN, LOWESTOFT LOUNGE LIZARDS

LITTLE GEM: Just occasionally, a Pallas's warbler will set the pulses racing, perhaps in the bushes near Minsmere Sluice

Minsmere
A magical mosaic

N

WESTLETON

Dunwich Road

NATIONAL TRUST DUNWICH HEATH

Coastguard Cottages

SCOTT'S HALL

V **P** **T**

H **H**

H **H** **H**

THE SCRAPE

H

H

H

Minsmere River

The Sluice

To Leiston

EASTBRIDGE

Chapel

0		½		1	

1 km

0

miles

KEY:

	Dunes		Woodland & Scrub		Dry Grassland	**H**	Hide		Drainage Dykes
	Reserve Boundary		Heathland		Coastline	**V**	Visitor Centre/ Reception		Roads		Footpath
	Open Water		Arable Reversion		Lagoons with Nesting Islands	**P**	Parking		Byway		Visitor Trail
	Grazing Marsh/ Wet Grassland		Reedbed/Fen		Spring-sown arable	**T**	Toilet		Bridleway

Minsmere

Photo: CHRIS GOMERSALL, rspb-images.com

BRIGHTENING UP A WINTER'S DAY: Redwings call in during autumn and winter

RESERVE INFORMATION

Open dates

The reserve is open every day - except Tuesdays, Christmas Day and Boxing Day - from 9.00am to 9.00pm (or dusk if earlier).

The visitor centre is open from 9.00am to 5.00pm (February to October) or 4.00pm (November to January).

A public viewpoint overlooking The Scrape is always open and accessible from the beach.

Many parts of the reserve can be viewed from the extensive network of public rights of way in the area.

How to get there

From the north or west follow the brown tourist signs from the A12 at Blythburgh, or at Yoxford via Westleton. From the south, leave the B1119 just north of Leiston and enter the reserve via Eastbridge.

Further Information

For further information, please contact:

RSPB Minsmere Nature Reserve, Westleton, Saxmundham, Suffolk IP17 3BY.

Tel: **01728 648281**. email:**minsmere@rspb.org.uk**

Facilities

- Visitor centre with education room, shop, tea-room and toilets

- Two visitor trails, each 1.5 miles (2.4km) long. Allow 2 hours for each one

- Eight hides along the trails, four of them with special low-level viewing slots for wheelchair users

- At present the majority of the trails are only passable by wheelchairs and pushchairs with difficulty. Improvements are being made

- Programme of guided walks and family events.

Cost

ADULT:	
RSPB members	FREE
Non-members	£5.00
CHILDREN (UNDER 16):	
RSPB members	FREE
Non-members	£2.50
Concessionary	£3.00
FAMILY TICKET:	
Up to 2 Adults & 4 Children	£10.00

Havergate
Island of the avocet

Main photo: JOHN KERR/ EVENING STAR, IPSWICH

AVOCETS: The island's special species

Geography and history

Havergate, Suffolk's only island, lies in a stretch of the River Ore estuary that was once open sea. More than 1,000 years' accumulation of sand and shingle has formed the spit of land we now call Orfordness and which encloses Havergate in the long, narrow estuary running from Aldeburgh to Shingle Street.

Havergate today is a little under two miles long and covers 108 hectares (265 acres). It consists of two original islands joined by a shingle bank and is covered mainly by shallow lagoons containing small islands and mudflats for breeding birds, and wintering wildfowl and waders.

Although below sea level and at risk from flooding by the increasingly high tides, it is protected by river walls first begun by local people over 500 years ago. Inside these, farmers were able to drain and improve the land. There is evidence from the ridge and furrow patterns still visible in some of the lagoons that crops such as vegetables and corn were grown, but cattle-grazing became the prime use. The cattle were brought over by a barge, half of which is still visible on Orford Quay, to the north end of the island.

The remains of a cottage and garden, where the farmers and their families lived, could be seen until recently. We know from records and local memories that the Brinkley family, and then a Mr Welham and his housekeeper, lived in a cottage on the island from 1865 to the late 1920s when they were employees of the then owner, a Mr Fiske. Faded photographs from before the Second World War show members of the Fiske family outside the cottage. Throughout the 1930s cattle were still brought to the island for summer grazing and then, in 1933, a gravel company began to exploit Havergate as a source of shingle, removing part of the shingle ridge joining the two halves of the island.

Smugglers took advantage of the island's isolation. Local folklore tells of the Havergate shepherd in league with smugglers who signalled with lights in the cottage window that the coast was clear for them to land their contraband on the deserted Ness and ferry illicit goods onto the island. After such a landing the shepherd would drive his sheep up and down on the foreshore to hide the tell-tale signs of activity. The Jolly Sailor Inn, near Orford Quay, still displays a poster, dated March 26, 1800, offering £20.00 for the capture of the Suffolk maidservant Margaret Catchpole who fell in love with one of the smugglers and, for his sake, stole a horse and rode it from Ipswich to London. By 1801 the unfortunate young woman had been caught, tried and transported to Australia.

Havergate

BIRD'S EYE VIEW:
An aerial view of Havergate
Island, looking south, with
the spit of Orfordness to the
left and Butley River running
off to the right near the
southern end of the island

Photo: MIKE PAGE

Havergate

The Second World War played a decisive role in the future of Havergate.

Situated near the most easterly point of England, the area's isolation was combined with vulnerability to attack and invasion. The result for Havergate was benign neglect. The land flooded with sea water, access for farm animals and people was denied, and a safe haven for breeding and wintering birds was created.

Avocets returned to breed on the island in 1947 after an absence from Britain of almost 100 years. The species had previously suffered persecution but the future for the avocet, and for all Havergate's wildlife, was assured by the RSPB's purchase of the island in 1948 - and the avocet became the society's emblem.

The purchase also began the association of the Partridge family with Havergate and its development as an RSPB reserve. Under the wardenships of Reg, his son John and their successors, Havergate has acquired an international reputation. It is a Grade 1 Site of Special Scientific Interest, a Grade 1 National Nature Reserve and is a Ramsar Site. It is in an Area of Outstanding Natural Beauty on the Suffolk Heritage Coast and is part of the Suffolk River Valleys Environmentally Sensitive Area.

Between 25 and 30 bird species breed here, including about 100 pairs of avocets. In any one year about 150 species are recorded. Rats, foxes and, above all, the weather have created problems and crises on the island. Hurricane force winds in 1953, 1983 and 1987 caused havoc, wrecking sea defences along the coast, submerging Havergate and breaching the river walls. A reminder of the 1953 storm is the marker post near the accommodation huts on the island showing the high-water mark of the floods. This is the highest point on the island, so the upperparts of the huts and the river wall were all that could be seen above the water.

At the height of this storm, warden Reg Partridge summoned his reserves of strength and experience to rescue in his small boat two security policemen from the Atomic Weapons Research Establishment who were stranded on Orfordness. He won the British Empire Medal for his courage.

The reserve has survived challenges such as these over the years thanks to heroic efforts by the Partridges and local volunteers, including those from the Woodbridge RSPB group. The river walls have been made wider and higher to cope with rising sea levels and hides have been refurbished and rebuilt.

Habitat management

Punctuated by these emergencies, the management and maintenance of the reserve as a major wetland area has continued.

There are now five hides overlooking the original fields of Havergate which have been transformed into six artificial lagoons with the deeper water at the edges marking the positions of the traditional 'borrow' dykes around each field. The clay dug from these ditches is 'borrowed' to make the sea walls. The mud in which waders and ducks feed in the lagoons is covered by about 15cm of sea water which flows through at each rise and fall of the tide and is controlled by sluice gates. Water salinity is monitored regularly to keep it close to the 3.5% salt and mineral content of the estuary and sea water, thus providing appropriate conditions for invertebrates such as *Corophium* shrimps, *Chironomus* midge larvae and ragworms, on which the birds feed.

Salinity in these shallow waters can vary dangerously, becoming diluted by heavy rain or more concentrated in hot weather due to evaporation. The salinity in Belper's lagoon is kept slightly lower, at 2.5%, by adding fresh water from a deep artesian well. This maintains the correct conditions for the extremely rare starlet sea anemone. The free circulation of sea water between the lagoons uses the system of ditches linked to the sluices. These need regular maintenance to clear the silt which accumulates from the estuary mud.

There are some 200 artificial shingle and mud islands in the lagoons. They provide nesting and roosting sites for waders, ducks and terns. The islands are covered in vegetation, such as couch grass, but erode gradually due to wave action and must be regularly rebuilt. Water levels are monitored to avoid flooding or drying out and are varied season by season for particular reasons. For example, the levels are raised slightly in winter, thus killing the vegetation on the island edges to create muddy or stony shores. The levels are kept high in spring to ensure the birds make their nests high on the islands and, once nest sites are established, the levels are dropped to reduce flooding risks in wet weather. In late spring the levels are dropped again to provide optimum feeding conditions for young and migrating birds.

Throughout autumn and winter, management work concentrates on creating ideal conditions for nesting and feeding on the islands. Islands accessible by tractor are mown in the autumn to provide a short growth for winter grazing of ducks and geese and to create the rough, short vegetation preferred as nesting sites by lapwings and redshanks the following spring. Some islands are left untouched to provide cover favoured by ducks such as mallards, shovelers and tufted ducks. Most islands, however, are completely cleared by cutting and pulling and some are rotovated because many wading birds, such as avocets, oystercatchers and ringed plovers - together with terns - prefer clear ground for their nests.

Although the lagoons and islands are the major habitats of the reserve, there is saltmarsh around the lagoons and around the island in a narrow band outside the river walls. The remains of the shingle bank which still links the southern, smaller island of Dovey's to the main island is an important site for rare spiders and plants.

DON'T WORRY: It's usually easier than this for visitors to disembark from the RSPB boat October Storm - there's a jetty along which they walk to shore.

Photo: JOHN KERR/ EVENING STAR, IPSWICH

Two small areas of gorse provide an important breeding habitat for linnets and, in winter, provide shelter for migrant species such as blackbird, robin, reed bunting and goldcrest.

With the threat of rising sea levels affecting this estuary site, the crumbling of the defences at the northern end of the island led to Havergate's contribution to 'managed realignment'. The sea wall was deliberately breached in 2000, flooding an area of grassland in Cuckold's Marsh so that saltmarsh could be restored. This project required complex planning - checking on existing water levels and drainage and listing existing flora and fauna - and follow-up survey work on accretion rates, erosion and changes in invertebrate populations.

Visitors will see that nature is taking its course, the tide sweeps in and out depositing mud, smoothing its surface, making new channels and flow patterns and creating new feeding areas for the probing beaks of waders. A biological succession will inevitably follow, with colonising plants on the highest banks trapping the mud and raising the land levels to create new saltmarsh - a habitat for breeding waders such as redshanks, and a natural defence against storm and flood.

BOXING CLEVER: Visitors are often pleasantly suprised to find the island has a colony of hares

Fauna

Brown hares were originally introduced to the island as a source of food. Now they number about 50. They are attractive to visitors and, as plant-eaters, are harmless to birds. Stoats, weasels, rats and foxes, however, are not so welcome as they prey on the eggs and young of nesting birds. Water voles and field voles, common shrews and water shrews have all been recorded and are the main diet of the short-eared owls that hunt the island's grasslands.

The most common of the 17 recorded species of butterfly is the Essex skipper. Other species regularly seen include small skipper, meadow brown, common blue, wall brown, red admiral, peacock and small tortoiseshell. In some years painted lady and clouded yellow butterflies arrive from Europe and settle on the island. Many other insects, including common darter and migrant hawker dragonflies, can be seen in summer, but the lack of freshwater pools prevents successful breeding.

The very localised ground lackey is among the moths on the reserve and on sunny days in late summer visitors may hear the hissing 'song' of the Röesel's bush cricket. The statlet sea anemone, invisible to the casual visitor but of international importance due to its rarity, is an extremely small mud-dwelling, brackish water invertebrate. It thrives at the edges of the lagoons, in small puddles in the mud made by the footprints of ducks and geese.

Flora

PURPLE HAZE: Sea lavender sets the island ablaze with colour, main photo. Inset, biting and English stonecrop, left, and sea campion add to Havergate's botanic interest and beauty

Main photo: JOHN PARTRIDGE, insets: KEITH BENNETT

The 134 species of plant on the island are typical of an estuarine habitat with clay soil, shingle, and high-level saltmarsh.

The most interesting are on the shingle bank south of the accommodation huts and on the high-level saltmarsh. In midsummer these areas abound in saltmarsh grass, scurvy grass, sea purslane, thrift, sea lavender and sea spurrey. On the shingle bank are herb robert, (yellow) biting stonecrop, English stonecrop, yellow vetch, sea campion, and the very localised sea pea. Sea wormwood can be found at the foot of the river banks and near Dovey's there are small patches of native cord grass.

The reserve has five species of marsh samphire and patches of reedbed. On the artificial mud and shingle islands in the lagoons the dominant plant is sea purslane which is interspersed with couch grass and patches of the invasive, woody and unattractive grass-leaved orache. The latter also grows in unwelcome profusion on the sea walls.

The Duke of Argyll's tea plant found on the island is perhaps a legacy from the old cottage garden and there is tamarisk which must also have been introduced at an earlier stage.

Birds season by season

WINTER: DECEMBER, JANUARY, FEBRUARY

The avocet may be the most famous of Havergate's birds with up to 700 now wintering, making the estuary an internationally important winter roosting site, but it is by no means the most numerous of the island's 150 species.

Every visitor has their favourite season on the island but most will agree that, for sheer numbers of birds, a winter visit never ceases to amaze and inspire. Between October and March large flocks of ducks and waders will be feeding in the lagoons, rising and wheeling round in huge numbers from time to time. A flock of avocets on Main or Dovey's lagoon disturbed by a predator such as a sparrowhawk can fill the air with a fluttering mass of black and white which settles again within minutes as a thin, distant black and white line. A cloud of dunlins flashing alternately light and dark can move low across the water and instantly vanish.

During these months there are seldom fewer than 400 or 500 wigeons present. Often, in the coldest part of the winter, the total is well over 2,000. Wigeon is usually the most numerous duck species, with teal a good second, but visitors may also expect to see up to 150 each of mallard, pintail and

Havergate

Main photo: KEITH BENNETT, inset, RSPB IMAGES

SILENT HUNTERS:
Short-eared owls hunt the island's grasslands. They have bred at Havergate

shoveler, while there are usually about 100 shelducks to be found on the island throughout the year. Wherever there is deeper water, such as in the ditches at the edges of the lagoons, groups of diving ducks can feed - tufted ducks, pochards and goldeneyes, with the occasional smew or scaup disappearing under the water with frustrating frequency.

There are enormous numbers of waders of between 10 and 15 species in winter, so some other interesting birds can be seen feeding or roosting alongside the avocets. Grey plovers are usually present in some numbers, together with knots, dunlins, common snipe, lapwings and redshanks. Barn owls are often seen in winter, even hunting in daylight. Short-eared owls visit from time to time and at least one hen harrier is usually around. A hovering kestrel is a common sight and, on the sluice gates, a perched kingfisher can often be seen.

Spring: March, April, May

Spring may start as early as February with the arrival of a few black-headed gulls and the first departures of the ducks. As the days lengthen, signs of the breeding season intensify with skylarks claiming their territory with song and redshanks gliding on vibrating wings in courtship flight.

The true excitements of spring can be seen in April as breeding birds migrate north from their winter feeding grounds further south in Europe, Africa or elsewhere. Fewer avocets will be seen here as some return to breeding grounds in mainland Europe. Elegant black-tailed and bar-tailed godwits, with the beginnings of their dramatic chestnut breeding plumage, may stay for a few days en route for breeding grounds in northern Europe and inside the Arctic Circle. Common, little and Sandwich terns will return before the end of the month and may be seen on the other side of the river wall, following the shallows of the river, hovering, diving and occasionally rising from the water with fish in their beaks. Later they may establish nests in the shingle on Havergate or at nearby sites such as Orfordness. Sometimes they are joined by two or three pairs of Arctic terns - Havergate is their most southerly breeding site in Britain.

Some breeding birds will be establishing their nest

MUD, GLORIOUS MUD:
It may look featureless, but every square inch of Havergate's mud teems with invertebrate life which sustains breeding and passage waders

PHOTO: JOHN PARTRIDGE

NATIONAL TREASURE: Havergate's avocets represent about 10% of the British population

sites with displays intended to drive away rivals and, at the same time, establish pair bonds with their mates.

Male shelducks engage in aggressive head-bobbing towards rival males whereas male avocets move from side to side around the female, dipping and splashing their upturned beaks through the water beside her as she submissively lowers her head. Oystercatchers defend their territories with shrill, far-carrying piping calls and display with their bright red beaks open and held downward. A frequent visitor in all seasons is the marsh harrier. At this time of year they may be nesting in nearby secluded areas, perhaps on Orfordness or in the upper reaches of the Butley River, and both males and females will visit to hunt for prey for themselves and for their nestlings.

Wheatears and whinchats are regular passage migrants commonly seen on Havergate, passing through on their way to northern upland areas of Britain and beyond.

Havergate is the breeding site for about 10% of the 1,000 pairs of British avocets. By May they will be incubating eggs at their nests on shingle ridges or mud islands on the two southern lagoons, Dovey's and Belper's. The nest is a sparsely lined scrape with four beige and brown mottled eggs, typical of waders, camouflaged as in all ground-nesting birds. Some late passage migrant species, such

REDSHANK: A common sight on the island

as whimbrel, greenshank, grey plover and turnstone, may still be encountered. By the end of May the saltmarsh and shingle will be covered in pink clumps of flowering thrift. The last stragglers of over-wintering ducks will have departed, though a few mallards and shovelers may stay to breed. The northward passage of swallows, swifts, sand martins and house martins builds to a peak during May and groups of them may be seen hawking for insects over the lagoons. As at all times of the year, grey herons can be seen catching eels and small fish in the ditches at the edges of the lagoons.

Photo: BILL BASTON

Photo: ANDREW EASTON/
LOWESTOFT LOUNGE LIZARDS

EXOTIC: Spoonbill, left, and little egret are two species which have become regular visitors to the island

SUMMER: JUNE, JULY, AUGUST

By June, the main interest centres on the breeding birds. Many of the avocets may now have young which are moved by the parents at a few days old from one lagoon to the next in search of the best feeding areas. The vulnerable chicks need vigorous protection by their parents against the predatory and voracious lesser black-backed and herring gulls.

It is possible to see the other waders which breed on or near Havergate - redshanks, ringed plovers, lapwings and oystercatchers - feeding in the lagoons or resting on the islands. The breeding success of these ground-nesting birds is very dependent on the weather and the number of predators. Gulls, the occasional fox or long periods of rain can cause a great deal of trouble. However, there will be few other waders apart from dunlins around at this time. To compensate, the smaller birds which nest on the island - meadow pipits, skylarks, linnets and reed buntings - should be much in evidence.

Photo: ANDY HAY/rspb-images.com

PASSING THROUGH, OR HERE FOR THE SUMMER: Havergate can be a busy place in summer. Turnstones, above, start appearing on their long distance migrations in August, a time when the island's common terns, inset, are still engaged in the business of raising young.

Photos: IAN PARADINE

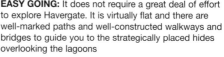

EASY GOING: It does not require a great deal of effort to explore Havergate. It is virtually flat and there are well-marked paths and well-constructed walkways and bridges to guide you to the strategically placed hides overlooking the lagoons

lenty of black-headed gulls breed on the island. Along with the lesser black-backed gulls breeding on Orfordness they contribute to the raucous noise which greets all visitors.

The picture changes again by July when many of the breeding birds will have chicks which will be almost fully grown. The increase in the numbers of breeding birds makes July one of the most interesting months on the island and it also sees the start of the southward wader migration. Dunlins and ringed plovers are on the increase, followed by turnstones, common sandpipers and knots and, by the end of the month, green sandpipers and greenshanks may also be seen. In

recent years, some more exotic species have spent time feeding in the lagoons, with small groups of little egrets and spoonbills making frequent visits at this time of year.

By August, the breeding season is virtually over but the breeding birds are still very much on view against a backdrop of the rich, purple colours of sea lavender. Avocet numbers peak in August and those from Havergate will be joined by adults and fledged young from other breeding grounds in Britain and Europe.

They will be resting in groups along with redshanks, oystercatchers and young shelducks, whose parents have moved away to moult.

DUNLIN: The most numerous small wader to pass through Havergate on autumn migration

The early stages of return passage conitunue with the arrival in the second half of the month of other migrants on their way south. Bar-tailed and black-tailed godwits, curlews, whimbrels, turnstones, knots, greenshanks, common sandpipers and golden plovers are often present, with one or two curlew sandpipers and the occasional little stint among the dunlins.

The arrival of grey plovers and the first wigeons ends the month and signifies the end of summer.

BLACK-TAILED GODWIT: A majestic wader often seen gracing Havergate's food-rich lagoons

SANDWICH TERN: This species has bred but can be seen more reliably as a passage migrant

Reserve reflections: special memories of Havergate

"Three Partridges"

❛ When the avocets were first recorded at Havergate, watchers set up a continuous guard on them. They camped in tents near today's living quarters. Two local men, a Mr Groves and a Mr Hornsby, were connected with the RSPB and formed a committee to oversee operations.

They employed Theo Harvey to ferry watchers to and from the island but after Theo died Mr Hornsby asked Reg Partridge to take over the job. A short time later Reg was taken on by the RSPB as full-time warden.

There were no voluntary wardens staying on the island in those early years so Reg and I would spend time there, particularly during the breeding season. My role was to greet visitors and look after them until Reg had moored the boat and come ashore.

The accommodation then was two very basic huts, one for living and cooking in, the other for sleeping. Cooking was done on two paraffin stoves and there were very few other comforts. Our son John would also stay during the summer holidays and the headmaster of the local school would let him join us at times during term time as he classed it as education. John spent many hours on the island with Reg, standing him in good stead when he took over the wardenship.

Things were a little 'ad-hoc' in those days. I remember during the Suez Crisis fuel was in short

Photo: JOHN PARTRIDGE

ISLAND MAN: Reg Partridge, Havergate's first warden

supply. When Reg got low on his ration he rigged up a sail on his boat and sailed to the reserve.

In the great floods of 1953 Reg and a band of local helpers spent days and days repairing sea wall breaches and I remember this was done by filling hundreds of sandbags by hand and carrying them into place. However, the job

was completed in time so that the avocets could safely nest during the summer.

My involvement with Havergate with Reg, then John, has spanned 55 years and has been very enjoyable. ❜

Ettie Partridge

AUTUMN: SEPTEMBER, OCTOBER, NOVEMBER

The yearly cycle is completed in September and October when the green stems of samphire develop their red autumnal colours, summer birds such as the terns depart and hirundines and other migrants pass through. Small flocks of goldfinches may arrive to feed on seeds of sea aster and thistle. Ducks increase in number, beginning with mallards and wigeons, followed by pintails, shovelers and teals.

Havergate's lagoons and islands are the perfect winter habitats for this rich variety of wetland birds.

Havergate
Island of the avocet

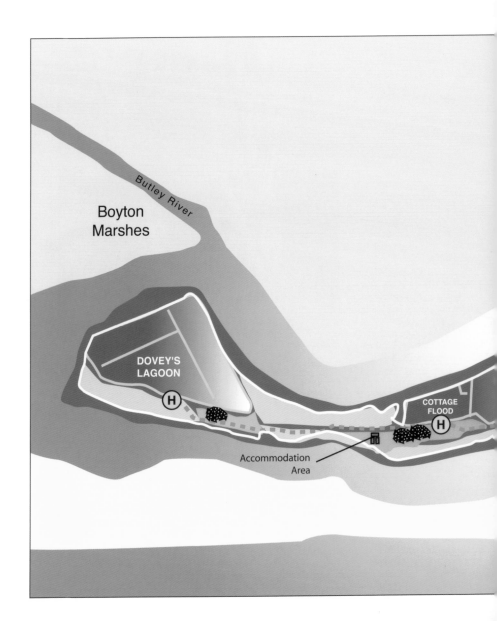

KEY:

Coastline	Gorse	**V** Visitor Centre/Reception
Vegetated Shingle	Lagoons with nesting islands	**L** Landing Stage
Saltmarsh	Permissive Footpath	**H** Hide
Rough Grassland	**T** Toilets	

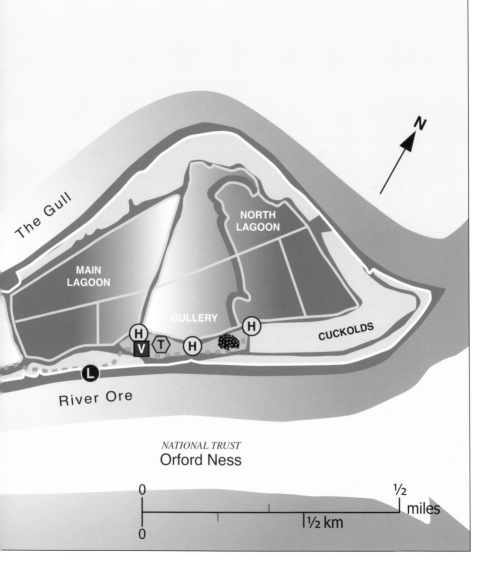

The Gull

NORTH LAGOON

MAIN LAGOON

GULLERY

CUCKOLDS

River Ore

NATIONAL TRUST
Orford Ness

0   ½

½ km   miles

0

Reserve reflections: special memories of Havergate

"Maintenance - a thumbnail sketch"

Enthusiasm for birds expresses itself in many ways; for those of us lucky enough to live near the enchanting Suffolk coast, where Minsmere and Havergate beckon, assisting wardens to manage these reserves is one rewarding option.

A hide repair work party was organised one February to replace unstable seating with benches.

The view from the hide we were working on was spellbinding - but work had to continue. Concentration was hard here with so much to see and then it happened! The darting flight of one of the island's latest arrivals distracted me and the hammer I was aiming at a monster nail missed and whacked my thumb instead! It was very painful, and black for many months, but the reward of seeing those birds was worth it.

Malcolm Key, *volunteer worker*

RESERVE INFORMATION

Open dates

The reserve is open from April to the end of August on the first and third weekends of the month and every Thursday. From September to March, the reserve is open on the first Saturday of the month.

The boat leaves Orford Quay at 10am and returns at 3pm.The journey takes about 20 minutes.

How to get there

Orford is located 17km (11 miles) north-east of Woodbridge. The village is signposted off the A12. Follow the A1152 and then the B1084 to Orford. There is a large pay-and-display car park near the quay.

How to book

There are limited places on the boat from Orford Quay, so prior booking is essential.

Bookings are taken through the visitor centre at the RSPB's Minsmere nature reserve, tel: 01728 648281, open from 9am-5pm (1 February-31 October) and from 9am-4pm (1 November-31 January) Closed Tuesdays.

Facilities

- Five birdwatching hides
- viewing platform
- visitor reception centre
- picnic area
- public toilets
- visitor trail of about 2km.

Wheelchair access is not possible.

Cost

ADULT:

RSPB members	£3.00
Non-members	£5.00

CHILDREN (UNDER 16):

RSPB Wildlife Explorers members	£1.50
Non-members	£2.50

Further information

If you would like more information about Havergate Island Reserve, please contact The Warden, e-mail ian.paradine@rspb.org.uk

Reserve reflections: special memories of Havergate

"Eyes like a hawk"

One of my most treasured memories from the early days was being there at the time when Reg Partridge was warden.

At that time the summer warden always had Tuesdays off and that was when Reg might take the voluntary for a spot of birdwatching (that's if he liked you - if he didn't, you would continue straightening nails, I joke not) I had been fortunate enough to find favour so my birdwatching was enhanced by a warden who probably had the best long sight in the business (why he bothered with binoculars I shall never know), but as we wandered round for the first time he said: "I like to find something on the summer warden's day off" and we always did - Reg had eyes like a hawk.

On one of these forays - it must have been in June - a spotted redshank in splendid summer plumage came over the bank and into the lagoon accompanied by a paler bird. I could identify the darker bird but the paler one was a puzzle so I asked Reg: "That's one of nature's little tricks. They're both duskies, one's in summer plumage and the other's in winter garb." (Reg always used dialect for birds).

Keith Bennett, *summer warden 1986 - 89*

Boyton Marshes
Beside Burrow Hill

QUIET CORNER: Boyton Marshes offer tranquility and good birdwatching. Barn owl, inset, is one of the reserve's specialities

Geography and history

The panorama of Butley Creek, with Boyton Marshes on its west bank, can be seen at its best from the summit of Burrow Hill. From here the creek and grazing marshes can be seen in the foreground and, stretching beyond them, the Ore estuary, Havergate Island, Orfordness and finally the open sea. This hill was occupied by Anglo Saxons - graves and domestic ware were recently discovered on the summit.

The landscape has changed over the centuries as farmers have built river walls and dykes to enclose, and then drain, the reedbeds and saltmarsh of the once expansive estuary. The Dutch engineers who probably built these walls in the 17th century used the traditional technique of excavating a dyke and using the 'borrowed' clay and mud to construct a parallel embankment on the seaward side. These 'borrow' dykes can be seen inside the river walls throughout the reserve.

From the Middle Ages to fairly recent times, Butley Creek was a busy waterway.

Corn was ferried upstream to Butley Mills and sailing barges would call at Boyton Dock, now a familiar landmark below the river wall. The dock was used from 1639 for the export of valuable white clay from a deposit on a neighbouring farm. This was taken to London, Holland and North America to be used in the manufacture of Delftware pottery. Some of the profits from this were used by the Warner family to support the Mary Warner Almshouses in the nearby village of Boyton. The dock was also used to receive coal from the north of England, to export straw to London for carriage horses and to bring in return a cargo of manure for the fields.

By the 19th century, the boats would have been Thames barges, a few of which are still used as pleasure boats on the local estuaries. Coprolite mineral deposits, rich in phosphate and used in the making of fertiliser, were dug locally and exported from the dock until 1857. The trade was then resurrected and continued to the late 1880s.

During the Second World War, the fields

Photo: JENNY JAMES

IMPRESSIVE VISTA: Burrow Hill looms large just outside the reserve and offers fine views

were used as a tank training ground. Concrete block houses still on the marshes are reminders of this austere time. Life-size models of tanks were pulled from one block house to another while being shot at by real tanks, giving the tank teams good target practice. Concrete foundations for the Nissen huts in which the tanks and ammunition were stored and the models were made can be seen at Banter's Barn near the reserve car park. Two of the Nissen huts remain. After the war, this was a quiet, forgotten corner. It was one of the few remaining lowland wet grassland sites in the area, frequented by walkers, fishermen and sailors.

The RSPB, which purchased the 57-hectare (175.5-acre) reserve in 1990, aims to maintain this remote tranquillity but also to improve the environment for birds and other wildlife. Since its purchase the reserve has been managed by the warden of Havergate Island, but has also been under the particular care of Honorary Warden Reg Etheridge. Help is given by a group of volunteers from Woodbridge RSPB group. The grazing marshes have been returned to traditional management - and the birds have flourished. This is a working reserve,

so there are no hides or facilities, except a small car park. The reserve can be explored by means of public footpaths. The surviving farm building, Banter's Barn at the reserve entrance, has been restored but several original timber-framed byres with pantile roofs have had to be demolished as the timbers were unsafe.

Photo: REG ETHERIDGE

TARGET PRACTICE: One of the block houses used in wartime training

Photo: SIMON PARKER, EAST ANGLIAN DAILY TIMES

Boyton Marshes

Habitats and management

The reserve is part of the Suffolk Coasts & Heaths Area of Outstanding Natural Beauty. It is also part of the Suffolk River Valleys Environmentally Sensitive Area. The reserve consists of grazing marshes, with an extensive network of drainage ditches, many of which contain patches of reedbed. Farmland rises gently to the west and the reserve is bordered to the east by the borrow dyke, the river wall, saltmarshes and the Butley River. Its northern boundary is the River Tang and to the south it extends to the Ore Estuary opposite Havergate Island.

Since 1990, the reserve's numbers of breeding and wintering birds have expanded year by year. A total of 168 species has now been recorded on the reserve, with up to 49 of these breeding each year. The key to this success is water-level management in the grazing marshes, adjusting them seasonally according to requirements. These low-lying water meadows are traversed by a system of drainage ditches which lead from the farmland and from a series of springs into the reed-lined borrow dykes and then, via the Tang River Sluice, into the estuary. At several points the water flow in the ditches is controlled by bunds, or earth banks, with connecting pipes whose upper ends are adjusted to the desired water level on each side.

During the winter, water levels are raised to create lagoons in several of the fields where wildfowl and waders can roost and feed on vegetation or on worms and other soil invertebrates.

From May to early November, the water levels are lowered and the short grass, needed to attract ground-nesting redshanks and lapwings, is maintained by a herd of about 100 cattle that graze the meadows in rotation, moving into fields as the ground-nesting birds complete their breeding. The rough, grassy sward is also grazed by Canada and greylag geese.

Photo: REG ETHERIDGE

Some fields are cut for hay and any remaining rushes or unwelcome thistles and nettles are mown in early autumn. The ditches are cleared one side at a time in rotation to maintain the water flow and drainage.

The saltmarshes and areas of estuarine mud are equally important feeding grounds for waders and wildfowl. Here, ducks such as teals and wigeons feed at low tide on seeds and insects in the saltmarsh vegetation and waders use their long beaks to probe the mud for invertebrates such as *Hydrobia* snails, *Corophium* shrimps, and ragworms. Future plans envisage systems for water storage to maintain water levels so that there are a few pools on the grazing meadows for summer and autumn passage migrants.

Flora

The range of flora on the reserve reflects the distinct habitats here. In the saltmarsh, characteristic plants such as fleshy green marsh samphire or glasswort, known also as poor man's asparagus, grow on the muddy margins and the pink thrift of early summer flowers on the drier parts. In July and August, the purple of sea lavender and sea aster creates a striking border to the muddy foreshore. On the river wall, clumps of shiny, spinach-like leaves of sea beet and the aromatic sea wormwood grow among the sea couch grass. The water-loving plants of the ditches flourish in the fresh water that moves steadily through to the borrow dykes. Many are reed-fringed and among the reeds forget-me-nots, water mint, yellow iris, figwort, purple loosestrife and the deadly hemlock all flower through the summer season. Beneath the water surface, water crowfoot leaves move in the slow current, its small white flowers projecting above the water.

Plants of light, sandy soils are often very localised. On the dry margins of the track down to the reserve the tiny white flowers of spring beauty, introduced from North America, cover the ground in spring. Beside the track leading to the river wall, dittander, an unusual coastal plant, can be seen. It has dense clusters of white flowers on robust stems.

Fauna

Most of the small mammals on the reserve – short-tailed field voles, water voles and wood mice - are well hidden from humans but are hunted for food by the resident barn owls and kestrels. Stoats and weasels can sometimes be seen as they scurry across the footpaths. Foxes, stalking along the hedgerows, are a common sight in the early morning and the occasional otter, badger and various deer may visit the reserve. There are rabbits in the drier areas, providing food for the foxes. In spring, hares attract our attention on the grazing marshes with their boxing displays. Common seals and occasionally grey seals venture into the river and may stay for several weeks, lying on the mud or simply

Photo: REG ETHERIDGE

PLANT LIFE: The reserve's rich flora includes marsh marigolds

Photo: DR. DAVID HEALEY

SPOT THIS: Four-spotted chasers can be seen on the reserve

popping their heads out of the water, revealing their large, round eyes.

In the borrow dykes and smaller ditches, frogs and toads deposit their spawn and eels and rudd, once caught by the local boys, now provide a good food supply for herons and cormorants. The dykes also provide places for dragonflies and damselflies to deposit their eggs on underwater plants. From June to August the adults emerge from the water to range and feed over wide territories. Southern hawkers, common darters and four-spotted chasers may be joined by migrant hawker dragonflies, together with common blue and large red damselflies.

On May evenings, clouds of delicate, ephemeral mayflies fly over the water surface trailing their paired tails' before mating and laying their eggs in the water. Along the river wall small tortoiseshell, meadow brown and gatekeeper butterflies can be seen on fine, warm days and ground lackey moths flutter low over the saltmarsh plants. Migrant painted ladies may rest on the ground when conditions are favourable and peacock butterflies can usually be seen feeding on the nectar of the bramble flowers.

Birds season by season

WINTER: DECEMBER, JANUARY, FEBRUARY

A walk along the sea wall in winter is a memorable experience. Up to 1000 wigeons and 600 teals may be feeding in compact flocks in the flooded areas of the grazing marshes. When disturbed they fly and wheel around, the wigeons' distinctive whistling calls and whirring wings being characteristic sounds of winter.

In the wet meadows to the south of the reserve, wigeons feed among the larger wintering wildfowl. Up to 40 mute swans, 200 greylag geese and 800 Canada geese regularly feed here. Occasionally they are joined by other goose species, such as tundra bean, brent, barnacle and white-front. Curlews, lapwings and common snipe can be seen on the reserve throughout most of the year but are here in much larger numbers in winter, with a few jack snipe joining them.

Resident gadwalls and tufted ducks can be seen alongside mallards, coots and moorhens on the borrow dykes. Looking towards the river by the dock, meadow

FINE SIGHT: Geese gather on one the reserve's winter floods

pipits, stonechats, rock pipits and occasional flocks of twites can be seen as they feed on seeds, insects and the numerous spiders among the saltmarsh plants.

Also from the dock, towards high tide, flocks of avocets can be seen flying up the estuary and returning as the ebb begins. On the mud, among the herring gulls and black-headed gulls, redshanks feed along the tide margins, occasionally taking flight and emitting their distinctive call. Small flocks of dunlins may appear, flickering dark and white before they also settle to feed. Ringed plovers scurry busily along the water's edge as small groups of knots rest on the mud and black-tailed godwits probe under the water with their long bills. On the estuary, little grebes, often with visiting goldeneyes and great-crested grebes, dive and resurface as they feed. Very occasionally a red-throated diver may stray into the river from the larger flocks out at sea and, after a North Sea storm, perhaps a little auk may also be seen.

The pair of barn owls that roost in Banter's Barn are well known to those who visit and

OLD FRIEND: Visitors are almost certain to see black-headed gulls around the reserve

work on the reserve. The sight of their pale shapes with wings flapping and gliding as they quarter the reeds and marshes at dusk on a winter's day never fails to excite. This rural part of Suffolk is an important area for barn owls. They like the dry climate and there are plenty of small mammals in the rough grasslands and reedbeds for easy hunting.

The other resident raptors, a pair of kestrels, hunt by day so the two species should not conflict, but on occasions when the barn owls are out early the kestrels will assert their priority by attacking the owls. Other raptors that hunt regularly over the reserve in winter are marsh harriers and hen harriers. Common buzzards, and occasionally a rough-legged buzzard, may be seen. Indeed, the area around Butley River has held wintering rough-legged buzzards in more than one recent year, as has nearby Orfordness. Boyton Marshes is a regular winter haunt of peregrine falcons. They fly powerfully to soar and stoop over the river, often capturing a wader in flight. The smaller merlin also visits the reserve, often hunting pipits over the saltmarsh.

WINTER SPECIALITY: One species which the visitor to Boyton Marshes is virtually certain to see during the winter is wigeon. The reserve and the neighbouring Butley River hold impressive flocks at this time of year

Photo: REG ETHERIDGE

Photo: REG ETHERIDGE

Boyton Marshes

Photo: REG ETHERIDGE

TOWARDS THE SEA: Visitors are greeted with this fine view of Banter's Barn, the wartime buildings, and parts of Butley River and Orfordness as they approach the reserve from Dock Lane

SPRING: MARCH, APRIL, MAY

The first sign of spring is often groups of redwings, fieldfares and starlings gathering on the grazing marshes before their departure over the North Sea. Oystercatchers, which choose neighbouring estuaries for their winter feeding, return to the saltmarshes by early March. The wildfowl will also be decreasing in numbers as they leave for their breeding grounds to the north. This is also the time when the first summer migrants appear, perhaps a wheatear may bound ahead of the walker on the river wall or a party of sand martins may dash overhead. The kestrels respond to the increasing warmth and day-length with aerial displays as they glide and circle together in anticipation of mating and egg-laying. Water rails may emit their shrill screams from the depths of the reeds. Stock doves take advantage of the owl-windows on the gable ends of Banter's Barn to gain access to the building in which they construct their nests.

By April, many passage migrants visit the reserve pausing to feed and rest on the flooded fields or on the saltmarsh and mud beyond the river wall. Passage waders encountered at this time may include greenshanks, ringed plovers, spotted redshanks, whimbrels and green, common

Photo: REG ETHERIDGE

ON A CLEAR DAY: A bright, early spring day on the reserve and occasionally wood sandpipers. Chiffchaffs are usually the first of the breeding songbirds to be heard among the trees, followed by blackcaps and garden warblers, with sedge warblers, whitethroats and lesser whitethroats in the scrubby brambles and hawthorns.

Yellow wagtails will return to breed in the grasslands and reed warblers will be nest-building in the reeds, wary of the parasitic cuckoos searching for nests in which to lay their eggs. Resident corn buntings and reed buntings nest in the scrub and reeds. Swallows return to feed over the insect-rich meadows and the wartime block houses provide perfect nesting sites for them. Sand martins and house martins feed constantly over the reserve, joined in early May by swifts.

It is very satisfying for Honorary Warden Reg Etheridge and his volunteer helpers that lapwings and redshanks have increased year by year, so that there are now about eight breeding pairs of the former and four of the latter. Five or six pairs of skylarks breed in the drier fields. Such success is due to careful management of the grazing meadows to give areas of smooth, short grass for lapwings - which prefer to have

CACOPHONY: Sedge warblers sing their super-charged song from many points around the marshes

unbroken views from their nests - and tussocks and clumps of rushes to provide the slightly raised and protected nest sites preferred by redshanks. These ground-nesting birds have most to fear from the increasingly common carrion crows which feed on their eggs and young.

Another success story for the reserve is the increasing numbers of breeding waterbirds, including four pairs of gadwall and tufted duck, as well as the more numerous mallards, coots, moorhens and little grebes.

SPLASH OF COLOUR: Yellow wagtails, with their beautiful colours and bright, cheerful calls, are welcome spring visitors to the reserve, some staying on to breed in the grasslands

Photo: ANDREW EASTON/LOWESTOFT LOUNGE LIZARDS

LITTLE BIG-HEAD: Little grebes are numerous in the reserve's dyke system

SUMMER: JUNE, JULY, AUGUST

Through the early summer the kestrels and barn owls hunt and feed their young on the plentiful small mammals. Sparrowhawks will often be seen as they fly fast along the hedgerows and the characteristic silhouette of a little owl, a species that also nests on the reserve, may be picked out on one of the fence posts. By July, the young kestrels will have left their nest, the brood of up to three young staying with their parents who bring food to them as they perch in the hedges. In contrast, the three to five young that the barn owls rear each year are coaxed from the nest by the parents and then forced to leave their territory.

From the river wall, little and common terns can be seen patrolling the shallower waters and then hovering and plunging in to emerge with small fish. Dashing hobbies can be seen hawking over the grazing meadows.

Most of the songbirds will be silent and by this time the screaming swifts and their young will be on the point of departure. Returning migrants begin to arrive - first greenshanks, followed by wood, green and common sandpipers and then larger groups of curlews and black-tailed godwits. Their length of stay depends on the water levels, as earthworms and other soil invertebrates will be nearer the surface when the soil is damp.

AUTUMN: SEPTEMBER, OCTOBER, NOVEMBER

Autumn begins slowly on the Suffolk coast. Even if the weather is still fine and dry the numbers of waders feeding on the reserve increases steadily. The birds are able to move to the grazing meadows as the tide rises to cover the mud and then return to the estuary as the tide goes out.

Passerine migrants may be present in the areas of scrub and hedgerow, particularly when the wind blows in from the east.

Photo: REG ETHERIDGE

SALTMARSH: Large numbers of waders use this area of the reserve

During one such period, Suffolk's first isabelline shrike was found near Banter's Barn and attracted many admirers. Diligent searches of the reserve may well turn up other exciting vagrants at this time of year. By the end of the autumn, remarkably large numbers of birds are feeding on the estuary or on the reserve.

About 250 curlews, up to 300 redshanks, 300 lapwings, substantial numbers of black-tailed godwits and a few knots and ringed plovers may be involved in this build-up. The occasional pintail or shoveler may be picked out among the large numbers of wigeons and teals arriving for the winter on the grazing marshes.

Boyton Marshes

Reserve reflections: special memories of Boyton Marshes

"Looking back at Boyton"

❛ Boyton Marshes were part of Dock Farm up to the 1930s and my grandfather worked on the farm for Mr Minter. He would recall how, in the early years of the century, the dock was busy with shipping. In the days before the local roads were properly surfaced this was the common means of transportation. Grain and cattle were shipped off the dock and coal, seeds and general provisions were brought in.

By the time that I, as a young girl in the 1930s, walked the marshes the dock was no longer used for commercial trade. I lived in Butley at the time and we thought nothing of walking to Boyton Marshes and back to collect samphire which we would pickle in vinegar and use as a salad with cold meat. In autumn the fields were dotted with mushrooms and we would collect basketfuls and take them home to fry.

During the war I moved away to Hertfordshire, in service, and when I came back to visit relatives I found that I could not get down to the marshes as they had been taken over by the Army. You can still see some of their buildings and gun and searchlight emplacements.

Seven years ago I returned to my roots. I live in the Mary Warner Almshouses in the village and I love walking the marshes. On the dock I have put a seat which is for the use of anyone who, like me, just enjoys resting and watching the birds in this beautiful and tranquil place. ❜

Mrs Mary Chittock, née Foreman

Boyton Marshes
Beside Burrow Hill

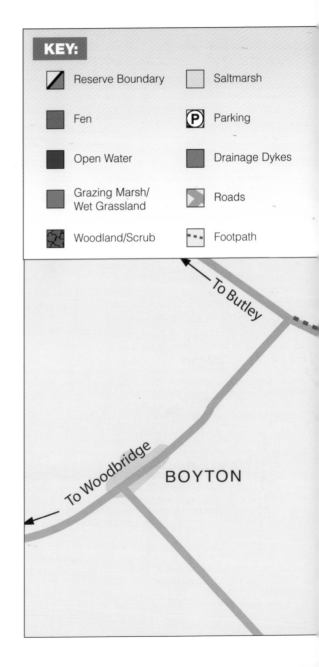

KEY:

▨	Reserve Boundary	▢	Saltmarsh
▨	Fen	Ⓟ	Parking
▨	Open Water	▨	Drainage Dykes
▨	Grazing Marsh/ Wet Grassland	▸	Roads
▨	Woodland/Scrub	⋯	Footpath

To Butley

To Woodbridge

BOYTON

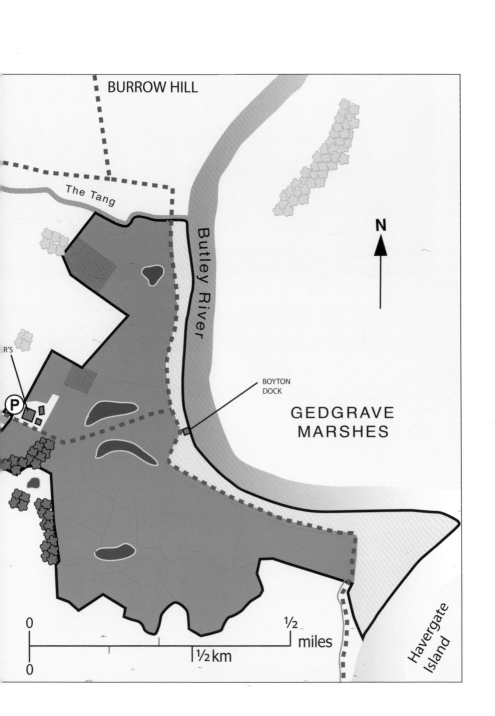

BURROW HILL

The Tang

Butley River

R'S

P

BOYTON
DOCK

GEDGRAVE
MARSHES

N

0

½

miles

½km

0

Havergate
Island

Boyton Marshes

Photo: MIKE RICHARDS rspb-images.com

BOLT OF BLUE: Kingfishers are often seen dashing along the reserve's dykes

RESERVE INFORMATION

How to get there

Take the A1152 from Woodbridge and then the B1084 to Butley. Turn right at the Oyster Inn, follow the road and turn left by the sculpture of St Andrew on the farm wall at the Capel St Andrew crossroads. At the first right-angle bend, follow the road to the right, at the second go straight on down a farm track towards the estuary. The car park is 300m down the concrete road, just before the barn.

Opening times

Access at all times, on public footpaths only.

Further information

If you would like more information about Boyton Marshes Reserve, please contact The Havergate Warden, e-mail ian.paradine@rspb.org.uk

HARD-WORKING HERD: About 100 head of cattle graze the meadows to maintain short grass needed by ground-nesting birds

Photo: REG ETHERIDGE

Dingle Marshes
A pioneering partnership

RSPB

Suffolk Wildlife Trust

Main photo: ALAN MILLER, inset CHRIS GOMERSALL, rspb-images.com

FRAGILE BEAUTY: The North Sea is just yards away from the marshes, which are home to the exciting marsh harrier, inset. The area is sometimes flooded by salt water

Geography and history

The area of lonely marshland and reedbeds north of Dunwich, known as Dingle Marshes, is steeped in history. One thousand years ago the present marshes formed the shore of a wide bay - Dunwich Haven - with the thriving city of Dunwich and its busy harbour on its southern margin. In the 12th century, Dunwich was one of the major east coast ports but since then the soft sandstone on which the city was built has been eroded progressively by the encroaching North Sea, taking houses, public buildings and 19 churches under the waves.

Now all that remains of the medieval city are the ruins of the Greyfriars Monastery outside the town walls on the present cliff edge and the chapel of the leper hospital in the churchyard of St James' Church at the end of the village street. The few remaining fishing boats and fishermen's huts on the beach are relics of its rich maritime history. The Dunwich River is reduced to a slow stream winding north through the marshes to join the River Blyth at Walberswick.

As the sea encroached and the bay silted up, enclosed by a natural shingle ridge, much of the low-lying ground became farmland used for rough grazing. Rising ground to the west remained as Sandling heath.

Between the wars, much of the heathland was planted with conifers by the Forestry Commission, to create Dunwich Forest. At the start of the Second World War, some of the water meadows were flooded as a defence measure and, as at Minsmere, the land reverted to reedbed. Much of this remains today and the northern part - Westwood Marshes - is managed as a reserve by English Nature.

The Dingle Bird Club was formed in 1954 and still exists. Its members study the migration of birds on the Suffolk coast. Their activities centre around bird-ringing on the Great and Little Dingle Hills, well-known landfall sites for migrating passerines. Mist nets have replaced the original Heligoland trap.

The Dingle Marshes Reserve of 258 hectares (637 acres) is a co-operative venture. It was purchased by the RSPB and Suffolk Wildlife Trust (SWT) in 1998 and is

NORTH FROM DUNWICH: Dingle Marshes, in all their glory, from the skies

jointly managed with a warden from each organisation in conjunction with English Nature, the Forestry Commission and Dunwich Town Trust. It consists of two contiguous main sections. One is the grazing marshes, with the Dunwich River and saline lagoons inside the shingle sea wall to the east. The other, to the north, is a thin segment of the wide valley of the Westwood Marshes reedbed which runs inland from the ruined windmill.

The acquisition of this reserve formed another link in the chain of coastal wetlands with saltmarsh, reedbeds and lagoons being conserved for wildlife along the Suffolk coast from Lowestoft to Felixstowe. This enables birds and other wildlife to move freely along 'corridors' between different feeding grounds and breeding sites, according to the season. The site was designated a National Nature Reserve in 2003. It forms part of the Suffolk Coast National Nature Reserve which encompasses 982 hectares of land from Dingle Marshes in the south to the Hen Reedbeds on the north side of the River Blyth.

Dingle Marshes is a quiet and remote reserve, deliberately low key, where visitors can use public and permissive footpaths to observe the wildlife in its natural habitat There is one hide overlooking the reedbed, with access through Forestry Commission land in Dunwich Forest.

EASY ACCESS:
Explorers of the marshes can set out from the beach car park signposted from Dunwich village. It is free but donations to the local church are requested

Habitats and management

The reserve is situated in the Suffolk Coast & Heaths Area of Outstanding Natural Beauty and is part of the Suffolk River Valleys Environmentally Sensitive Area. The marvellous qualities of the area have been recognised by the wide range of national and international designations applying to the site. It is a Site of Special Scientific Interest, a Special Protection Area, a Special Area of Conservation and a Ramsar site.

The management of Dingle Marshes is perpetuating wildlife-friendly farming methods in the grazing marshes and continuing co-operation with English Nature in Westwood Marshes.

The range of habitats - lowland wet grassland, reedbed, coastal lagoons, saltmarsh, vegetated shingle ridge, woodland and arable - creates the varied conditions which attract 60 species of breeding birds. The site has outstanding potential for all its wildlife to flourish and increase further in diversity in conjunction with suitable management techniques.

Rising sea levels and the historically unstable coastline pose problems for the

PREDATOR: Short-eared owls can be seen as winter visitors and passage migrants

Photo: ANDREW EASTON/ LOWESTOFT LOUNGE LIZARDS

reserve and the SWT and RSPB wardens. During most winters the soft sandstone cliff is further eroded and the shingle bank sea wall is breached. The sea floods into the reserve, causing damage to the populations of freshwater invertebrates and fish.

It will be important to plan ahead, creating new reedbeds and grazing marshes at locations further inland, to replace those which will inevitably be lost when maintaining the sea wall is no longer possible.

Dingle Marshes

Photo: PAUL GREEN

THE CRUEL SEA: In the aftermath of a ferocious winter storm, the shingle bank lies breached and Dingle Marshes suffer serious flooding once again

SEA OF GOLD: The Dingle Marshes reedbed makes a fine sight under wide blue skies

Reedbed

The Dingle Marshes reedbed is the southern part of Westwood Marshes - the largest freshwater reedbed in England. The larger northern part has been managed since 1972 by English Nature and the acquisition of the southern part by SWT and the RSPB allows the area to be considered as a single ecological unit and will be considered as such in this account.

It has developed on marine clays overlain by a thick layer of peat. Looking out over the vast expanses of reeds stretching into the distance, traces of its history can be detected - old gateposts, field boundaries, hedges and ditches survive from its time as grazing pasture. The marsh supports a specialist community of insects, birds and animals in the mixture of habitats provided by the reeds, the willow and alder fen, the ditches and lagoons. Marsh harriers, bearded tits and bitterns have maintained a presence here for many years and the planned management programme aims to sustain and enhance this. The reedbed has been traditionally managed with some of the reeds used for thatching.

NEAR NEIGHBOUR: Part of Walberswick's Westwood Marshes

The reeds are cut between November and January after the water levels have been lowered for access. Excess dead leaf litter is always raked and burned. Specific sectors are cut annually for a period of seven to ten years and then left while other areas are exploited. Certain areas of the reedbed are left for the Polish Konik horses from SWT's herd that thrives by grazing on the rough, wet vegetation. This harvesting, grazing and trampling prevents scrub encroachment and drying out and maintains a good flow of fresh spring water and surface drainage water through the reedbed and lagoons to the Dunwich River.

The 1930s drainage ditches have been opened up and widened to create 5m-wide water channels. This has already been successful in providing reedbed edges for feeding bitterns. It has also increased the area of open water for wintering and resident wildfowl. The reedbed has some protection from potential sea incursions thanks to a secondary earth dam with sluices, inland from the old windmill.

Grazing marshes

The view north over the grazing marshes from Dunwich village street must have remained virtually unchanged for hundreds of years. In summer, cattle graze in the meadows with swallows and house martins swooping for flies overhead. In winter, ducks and geese roost as the occasional visiting hen harrier quarters the reeds. The management plan revolves around keeping water levels higher in the silt and clay soils than in the recent past, using a series of sluices. Some of the original creeks have been opened up with mechanical diggers to increase the flow of fresh spring water flushing through any salt that may have accumulated and to provide more feeding edges for waders.

The vegetated edges of the ditches are a favoured habitat for nesting mallards and other ducks as well as numerous insects, amphibians and small mammals. A new Scrape, with islands for nesting waders, has been created by the Dunwich Beach car park. The pasture is kept well grazed by around 250 cattle in the summer months. They are moved from field to field to avoid the nesting birds. Rushes in the wet fields and ragwort in the dry fields are mechanically cut to prevent their spread. This creates the mosaic of short grass and tussocks favoured for nesting by lapwings and redshanks respectively.

Dingle Marshes

Dingle Marshes

DINGLE SHINGLE: The sweep of Sole Bay, looking towards Walberswick and Southwold

Coastline

The history of this coast is one of constant change, with natural movements of sand and shingle. The action of the sea creates a frequently changing profile to the shingle ridge. This needs to be regularly strengthened by bulldozing material from the beach to repair the damage caused by tidal surges and wave action.

The Dunwich River creates a barrier between fresh and salt water as it runs north, parallel to the sea wall. There are small patches of reedbed and scrub on its banks providing ideal habitats for nesting birds such as common whitethroats, sedge warblers, grasshopper warblers and reed warblers. An interesting and rare habitat can be seen between the river and the sea wall. Daily seepage of seawater has created saline lagoons surrounded by saltmarsh and shingle that has periodically been washed over the sea wall. Unusual invertebrates occur here - scarce brackish water *Gammarus* shrimps, and the rare starlet sea anemones alongside the abundant minute *Hydrobia* snails which provide food for the waders which nest on

the shingle. These parts are fenced off in the breeding season to ensure that the public keeps to the permissive footpath close to the sea wall.

WELCOME: An information board near Walberswick tells visitors about the reserve

Farmland and woodland

The small amount of arable farmland and woodland on the reserve is mostly situated on the gently rising ground formed by the sand and gravel post-glacial deposits of the Sandlings. There is a small section of marshy woodland in Fen Covert. The mixed deciduous woodland needs little management but the arable farmland is being reverted back to grassland and heath to encourage breeding and wintering woodlarks and skylarks. Some of the fields are being grazed by sheep and cattle as a first step, and others have been sown with seed-bearing crops such as linseed and millet as winter food for linnets, greenfinches and reed buntings.

Photo: DR. DAVID HEALEY

SUMMER SIGHTINGS: Dragonflies, such as the four-spotted chaser, can be seen on the reserve

Photo: TERRY WHITTAKER, THE WILDLIFE TRUSTS

SURVIVING: Water voles still inhabit the ditches on Dingle Marshes, despite a national decline in numbers

Fauna

A varied series of habitats such as this will inevitably support a wide range of other animal species besides birds. Otters have taken advantage of the solitude and plentiful supplies of rudd and eels in the reedbed, water voles and water shrews live in the ditches despite the occasional predatory mink. Muntjac stray in from the Dunwich Forest and red deer pass through on their way to the reedbed where they create useful tracks, breaking up the dense reeds. Hares can be seen bounding over the grazing marshes, badgers and rabbits burrow easily in the light, sandy soil in the south part of the reserve and on warm spring days adders and common lizards may be detected basking in the sunshine on the path edges. Grass snakes and amphibians such as toads, frogs and smooth newts have ample territory in the extensive reedbed. Foxes are kept out of the grazing marshes during the breeding season by electric fencing, thus protecting the eggs and young of the ground-nesting birds.

As expected in this traditional lowland environment, insect life flourishes. Butterflies such as common blue, holly blue and tortoiseshell can be seen feeding on the nectar of flowers at the edges of the tracks, the migrant painted lady appears in substantial numbers when conditions are favourable and speckled wood butterflies rest on vegetation on the woodland margins. Several species of dragonfly and damselfly can be seen flying in summer as they hatch from their aquatic larval stages in the ditches and pools. Hairy dragonflies are followed by southern hawkers and these may be joined by migrant hawkers and four-spotted chasers. The rare Norfolk hawker dragonfly is an increasingly frequent visitor and common blue, blue-tailed and large red damselflies can all be seen in the summer months. A large number of moths have been recorded on the reserve, among them the rare Fenn's wainscot.

Photo: ALAN MILLER

Photo: ALAN MILLER

SUMMER HIGHLIGHTS: Common lizards can be seen basking in the sunshine and, left, silver-studded blue butterflies are among the reserve's attractions

Flora

The most numerous plants on the reserve are adapted to wetland conditions. The huge expanse of reeds in the marshes, changing colour from green to purple and then brown and cream as the seed-heads develop and ripen, is a spectacular sight through the seasons. Other water plants, such as reed mace and the scarce marsh sowthistle, grow among the reeds. Spearwort, forget-me-not and arrowhead grow around the wetland margins and frogbit and bladderwort occur in the ditches. In the saltmarsh around the saline lagoons, the purple sea aster flowers in July and August. The shingle bank of the sea wall supports patches of rare but locally flourishing shingle loving plants - the pink sea pea, yellow horned poppy and sea kale. Oaks, sycamores and birch dominate the woodland with alder in the wet areas of Fen Covert and willow scrub along the edges of the reedbed.

Birds season by season

WINTER: DECEMBER, JANUARY, FEBRUARY

The Dingle Marshes reserve contributes to the network of wetlands on the Suffolk coast that provide havens for wintering wildfowl. It provides an alternative feeding area for many waders when the tide is high on the neighbouring River Blyth estuary. The wet grassland of the grazing marshes provides ideal feeding conditions for ducks and geese which winter here. They are best viewed from the beach car park, from the sea wall or from the Dingle track along the edge of Dunwich Forest. Up to 1000 teals

Photo: TIM BROWN/ LOWESTOFT LOUNGE LIZARDS

THERE'S NO BUNTING LIKE SNOW BUNTINGS: They are regular winter visitors to the beach area

...ay be feeding on seeds in the tussocky ...egetation with perhaps 500 to 600 ...igeons alongside them and smaller ...umbers of shelducks, mallards and ...hovelers. Greylag and Canada geese can ...e seen in all seasons, but they are joined ...n winter by varying numbers of white-...onted geese.

...locks of herring gulls and lesser ...black-backed gulls will visit to feed ...and roost, together with up to 400 ...pwings and groups of redshanks. Smaller ...umbers of common snipe, and ...ccasionally spotted redshanks, also ...inter here and can often be picked out as ...ey fly over the pools and ditches. On the ...hingle alongside the saline lagoons ...rnstones will feed and move on, their ...rtoiseshell plumage being an attractive ...ature of the winter scene. A regular flock ...f twites, sometimes numbering up to 70 ...rds, feeds on seeds on the shingle and ...nets, goldfinches and snow buntings can ...equently be seen among them. From the ...ide looking over the reedbed, several ...arsh harriers can often be picked out as ...ey hunt for amphibians or small ...ammals. In the winter months, they may ...e joined here in the reeds at dusk by other ...ptors such as hen harriers and merlins in ...e 'raptor roost'. With the aid of a ...lescope, the keen sea-watcher may be

able to pick out some of Sole Bay's wintering red-throated divers and great crested grebes.

SPRING: MARCH, APRIL, MAY

The departure of a flock of wintering ducks or geese, or a booming male bittern on a cold February morning, signals the change of season. The number of 'boomers' has increased - a clear response to the reedbed management programme. Maintaining these numbers will depend on the continued supply of freshwater fish and amphibians in the reedbed as food for the developing young birds.

The majority of the lapwings will have departed for their Continental breeding grounds by the end of March, but the 12 or so pairs which remain will be beginning their courtship displays to establish their territories in the grazing marshes. Redwings and fieldfares gather on the fields before flying north, coinciding with ring ouzels on their return to the uplands of Britain for the breeding season. The soaring song of the skylark, the piping display calls of redshanks and the arrival of the passage migrant waders confirms the arrival of spring.

Dingle Marshes

Photo: CHRIS GOMERSALL,
rspb-images.com

EXCITING SIGHT: Marsh harriers are a prominent feature of the reserve

From late March, common and green sandpipers and greenshanks will stay for a time on the edges of the pools in the grazing marshes before moving on. Ruffs, bar-tailed godwits and black-tailed godwits will follow, with turnstones on the shingle by the sea wall. By late April, grey plovers will be passing through and small groups of whimbrels may stay for a time feeding on the rich invertebrate life in the pastures. The bright plumage of the yellow wagtail attracts our attention on its way through, but pied wagtails can be seen more frequently as they breed on the reserve.

Of the 60 species of bird that breed on Dingle Marshes, none is more exciting to observe than the marsh harrier. At this time they will frequently be seen, performing their aerial displays, collecting nesting material or hunting over the reedbed. The males are polygamous, each one may mate with more than one female. In a good year there may be as many as ten females with nests in the Westwood Marshes reedbed, rearing over 20 young.

By contrast, water rails are rarely seen. It is estimated that there may be in excess of 100 pairs of this secretive species in 200 hectares of reedbed. Their squealing calls can be heard in the early morning from late March to mid-April, but their territories are only mapped with difficulty. The thick scrubby margins of the reedbed are used for nesting by the expanding resident population of Cetti's warblers. An explosive chatter reveals their presence as they feed at the water's edge.

On the broad expanse of the grazing marshes, the nesting lapwings and skylarks choose the open ground for the shallow nests. Redshanks prefer the cove of a tussock of rushes and gadwalls mallards, shovelers and tufted ducks see out the cover provided by the dens vegetation on the edges of the drainag ditches. Linnets and stonechats will begi to nest in the scattered patches of gorse o the higher areas.

Around the saline lagoons, ringed plovers avocets, oystercatchers and, occasionall little terns nest, their eggs we camouflaged against the mottled colours of the shingle stones. There are no gul breeding on the reserve, but their constar predatory forays cause considerabl losses among these ground-nesting birds as do those of the increasingly numerou carrion crows.

Most of the summer migrants will hav returned by the end of April and they will b establishing their territories, alongside th resident species. Reed buntings an bearded tits will be joined by sedg warblers, grasshopper warblers and ree warblers feeding and building the intricately woven nests in the reeds.

In the woodland and hedgerows, th territorial singing of songbirds such a blackcaps, garden warblers, willo warblers and chiffchaffs will be hear alongside resident robins, wrens bullfinches, song thrushes and blackbirds Common whitethroats and lesse whitethroats sing from the hawthorns an 'invisible' nightingales sing from the depth of dense vegetation. Green woodpecke call as they fly off the grassland and th drumming of great spotted woodpecke resonates through the woodland.

WINTER'S DAY: A light covering of snow creates a scene of beauty

SUMMER: JUNE, JULY, AUGUST

This must be the favourite time of year for many regular visitors to Dingle Marshes. On a still, warm day in mid-summer, looking across the reedbed from near the ruined windmill, families of bearded tits can be seen flitting through the tops of the reeds, feeding and calling as they move along. In the distance, a hobby may swoop and turn as it attempts to overtake and capture a dragonfly or damselfly over the water. From the sea wall common and little terns can be observed as they hover and plunge for fish in the sea or saline lagoons. As the dark brown young of the marsh harriers leave the nest they fly and hunt with their parents, but quickly become independent and competent hunters.

By late June, spotted redshanks, greenshanks, bar-tailed godwits, black-tailed godwits, dunlins, green sandpipers and the occasional little stint will be returning to the lagoons on the grazing marshes from breeding grounds further north. At the same time, any ringed plovers and oystercatchers that have bred will leave the reserve to feed on the local estuaries.

In June and July, an evening walk at dusk along the Dingle track might be rewarded with the sight of glow-worms in the short grass and the churring sound of nightjars as they hunt for moths through the clearings in the forest. Little egrets that breed locally can be seen on the reserve at all times of year, but from August onwards there can be as many as eight individuals feeding here, joined from time to time by a spoonbill.

AUTUMN: SEPTEMBER, OCTOBER, NOVEMBER

From September onwards, visitors may see redstarts and pied flycatchers stopping to rest and feed in areas of scrub on the reserve before these migrants move south. Large numbers of meadow pipits pass through during the autumn. Most are of Continental origin and are heading for their wintering areas on the Iberian Peninsula. Bearded tits gather into flocks early on October mornings and take off together, spiralling upward to disperse to other wetland areas in the south and west of Britain. Some bearded tits remain here in all months of the year but are vulnerable to hard weather and coastal flooding.

Month by month through the autumn, wintering wildfowl and waders will arrive from the north, gathering on the grazing marshes to roost and feed. There will be little disturbance. Few visitors other than naturalists and those seeking solitude come here in winter. The only sounds will be the crashing of waves on the shingle, the movement of the wind in the reeds and the trees of the forest, and the murmuring and whistling of the birds.

Dingle Marshes
A pioneering partnership

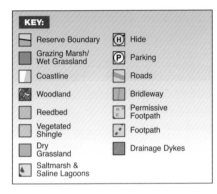

KEY:

	Reserve Boundary	H	Hide
	Grazing Marsh/ Wet Grassland	P	Parking
	Coastline		Roads
	Woodland		Bridleway
	Reedbed		Permissive Footpath
	Vegetated Shingle		Footpath
	Dry Grassland		Drainage Dykes
	Saltmarsh & Saline Lagoons		

Suffolk Wildlife Trust

To Blythburgh

DU
FO

0
½
1 km
0

GLISH NATURE
WOOD MARSHES

GREAT
DINGLE

LITTLE
DINGLE

To Walberswick

N

Dunwich River

℗ To Westleton

DUNWICH

Dingle Marshes

Reserve reflections: special memories of Dingle Marshes

John Brinkley Easy (may he rest in peace under the sea)

❝ My first encounter with John Brinkley Easy was in 1958. I came to Suffolk for the first time with a group of student birdwatching friends. We arrived late, in the dark, guided to the cliff-top campsite by one of our number who knew the area and who was to take us to Minsmere the next day. I pitched my tent and settled for the night in my sleeping bag on the hard ground. Then followed the most uncomfortable night of my life. Sinister dreams alternated with waking and listening fearfully to the sound of the sea below us. I woke as the sun rose out of the sea and saw the amazing view from our position perched on the cliff edge. Only then did I look to the side of the tent and see the solitary tombstone and the grave on which my tent was pitched.

There was the inscription:
*SACRED
To the Memory of
JOHN BRINKLEY EASY
1826
23Years*

When I returned to Dunwich 20 years later I discovered the story of Dunwich, the city under the sea, and the churchyard of All Saints' Church where John Easy had been buried. The grave was much nearer to the edge of the cliff as the waves and storms had taken their toll on the soft sandstone. Since then the tombstone and the cliff-top campsite have all been swept into the sea and I do not know what happened to John Brinkley Easy. ❞

Jenny James

A pioneering partnership

RESERVE INFORMATION

How to get there

From the A12 via Westleton or Blythburgh to Dunwich village

Opening times

Access at all times on public and permissive footpaths only

Facilities

- Car parks - recommended parking for the footpath to the hide: Dunwich Forest car park on the road between Dunwich and Blythburgh

- Information boards - Dunwich Beach car park; Dunwich Forest car park; Bridge Farm entrance to Dingle track; the reserve's northern boundary on the beach; near the ruined windmill.

- Hide - one hide overlooking Westwood Marshes with access through Dunwich Forest.

- Refreshments - café, tearoom and public house in Dunwich village.

- Toilets - beach car park

- Wheelchair access - Dingle track along the edge of the Dunwich Forest is firm but with an uneven surface. It may be muddy and rutted, particularly after wet weather.

Further information

If you would like more information about Dingle Marshes Reserve, please contact the SWT warden, tel:01728 833405, e-mail alanm@suffolkwildlife.cix.co.uk

GLOSSARY

DESIGNATION OF BIRD AREAS: *Each reserve has a number of statutory designations and these are listed in the chapters. Just the names do little to enlighten the reader as to the importance of such designations. The following explanations may help:*

AREA OF OUTSTANDING NATURAL BEAUTY (AONB)

Forty-one areas in England and Wales. Designated for the quality of their landscape by The Countryside Commission. The Suffolk Coast & Heaths AONB was designated in 1970. All the reserves featured in this book are within this area. AONBs have management plans that co-ordinate policy and action to conserve and enhance their character, flora and fauna.

COUNTRYSIDE STEWARDSHIP SCHEME (CSS)

Agri-environment scheme run by the Department of the Environment, Farming and Rural Affairs (Defra). Grants to landowners for environmentally sensitive management of their landholdings.

ENVIRONMENTALLY SENSITIVE AREA (ESA)

Agri-environment scheme run by Defra. Imposes conditions on the management of lowland wet grassland, as in the Suffolk River Valleys. There are grants given to support the opportunity cost of less intensive management. CSS and ESA are due to be amalgamated in 2005 into the new Environmental Stewardship Scheme.

COUNCIL OF EUROPE DIPLOMA

Recognition for the exceptional management of an area of European importance to conservation.

RAMSAR SITE

A wetland site of international importance designated under the conventions signed in Ramsar, Iran, in 1971. Signatory countries are required to formulate planning policies so that such sites are adequately conserved.

SPECIAL AREA OF CONSERVATION (SAC)

Derived from the EU Habitats Directive. Applied to areas of European importance with the objective of protecting threatened species of wildlife. The aim is to conserve natural habitats and wild flora and fauna of Community importance.

SPECIAL PROTECTION AREA (SPA)

Derived from the EU Birds Directive. Applied to areas of European importance. Requires special measures to conserve the habitat of listed bird species to ensure their survival and reproduction in their area of distribution.

SITE OF SPECIAL SCIENTIFIC INTEREST (SSSI)

Sites identified by English Nature on behalf of the UK Government. The purpose is to protect areas of national importance from damage or destruction. Such sites have to have management plans agreed by English Nature.

PUBLIC TRANSPORT

North Warren & Aldringham Walks

Rail: Nearest station is Saxmundham.
Buses: Service No. 64 Ipswich/Woodbridge/Leiston/Aldringham/Aldeburgh, Monday to Saturday only.
Sunday: Service No. 82A and 81A, as above, but also to Thorpeness.

Minsmere

Rail: Nearest station is Darsham.
Road: There is a taxi service planned, at bus rates, starting from Darsham Station in the summer of 2004. Call Traveline, 0870 6082608 for more information.

Havergate Island

Rail: Nearest station is Melton.
Buses: To Orford, Service Nos. 122/123/160/161/182 (Monday to Saturday only)
Boat: The boat from Orford to Havergate Island must be pre-booked by telephone, contact 01728 648281.
Bicycles: National Cycle Route No. 1 goes via Orford.

Boyton Marshes

Rail: Nearest station is Melton.
Buses: Service No. 160 from Woodbridge (Monday to Saturday only)

Dingle Marshes

Rail: Nearest station is Darsham.
Road: There is a taxi service planned, at bus rates, starting from Darsham Station and going to Dunwich, in the summer of 2004.
Call Traveline, 0870 6082608 for more information.

Travel telephone enquiries

For stations on the East Suffolk Railway Line, and information on the carriage of bicycles, call National Rail Enquiries on 08457 484950. For bus information call Traveline on 0870 6082608

Tick 'em off
A checklist of Suffolk birds

The following table enables observers to keep a 'ticklist' of species they have seen on the five reserves featured in this book. This is the official list and order of species recorded in Suffolk, as at June, 2004. The species names are those used by the British Ornithologists' Union and in some cases differ from those used in the text of this book, which adopts a more colloquial approach.

	NORTH WARREN & ALDRINGHAM WALKS	MINSMERE	HAVERGATE ISLAND	BOYTON MARSHES	DINGLE MARSHES
DIVERS					
RED-THROATED DIVER					
BLACK-THROATED DIVER					
GREAT NORTHERN DIVER					
YELLOW (WHITE)-BILLED DIVER					
GREBES					
LITTLE GREBE					
GREAT CRESTED GREBE					
RED-NECKED GREBE					
SLAVONIAN GREBE					
BLACK-NECKED GREBE					
TUBENOSES					
NORTHERN FULMAR					
CORY'S SHEARWATER					
GREAT SHEARWATER					
SOOTY SHEARWATER					
MANX SHEARWATER					
BALEARIC SHEARWATER					
LEACH'S STORM PETREL					
EUROPEAN STORM PETREL					
GANNETS					
NORTHERN GANNET					
CORMORANTS					
GREAT CORMORANT					
EUROPEAN SHAG					
HERONS					
GREAT BITTERN					
LITTLE BITTERN					
BLACK-CROWNED NIGHT HERON					
SQUACCO HERON					
CATTLE EGRET					
LITTLE EGRET					
GREAT (WHITE) EGRET					
GREY HERON					
PURPLE HERON					
BLACK STORK					
WHITE STORK					
GLOSSY IBIS					
EURASIAN SPOONBILL					
SWANS					
MUTE SWAN					

TUNDRA (BEWICK'S) SWAN	
WHOOPER SWAN	

GEESE

BEAN GOOSE (TUNDRA & TAIGA)	
PINK-FOOTED GOOSE	
GREATER WHITE-FRONTED GOOSE	
LESSER WHITE-FRONTED GOOSE	
GREYLAG GOOSE	
SNOW GOOSE	
CANADA GOOSE	
BARNACLE GOOSE	
BRENT GOOSE, inc. PALE BELLIED & BLACK BRANT	
EGYPTIAN GOOSE	
RED-BREASTED GOOSE	

DUCKS

RUDDY SHELDUCK	
COMMON SHELDUCK	
MANDARIN DUCK	
EURASIAN WIGEON	
AMERICAN WIGEON	
GADWALL	
COMMON TEAL	
GREEN-WINGED TEAL	
MALLARD	
NORTHERN PINTAIL	
GARGANEY	
BLUE-WINGED TEAL	
NORTHERN SHOVELER	
RED-CRESTED POCHARD	
COMMON POCHARD	
RING-NECKED DUCK	
FERRUGINOUS DUCK	
TUFTED DUCK	
GREATER SCAUP	
COMMON EIDER	
LONG-TAILED DUCK	
BLACK (COMMON) SCOTER	
VELVET SCOTER	
BUFFLEHEAD	
COMMON GOLDENEYE	
SMEW	
RED-BREASTED MERGANSER	
GOOSANDER	
RUDDY DUCK	

BIRDS OF PREY

EUROPEAN HONEY BUZZARD	
BLACK KITE	
RED KITE	
WHITE-TAILED EAGLE	
EURASIAN MARSH HARRIER	
HEN HARRIER	
MONTAGU'S HARRIER	
PALLID HARRIER	
NORTHERN GOSHAWK	
EURASIAN SPARROWHAWK	
COMMON BUZZARD	
ROUGH-LEGGED BUZZARD	
GREATER SPOTTED EAGLE	
OSPREY	
COMMON KESTREL	
RED-FOOTED FALCON	

MERLIN			
EURASIAN HOBBY			
GYR FALCON			
PEREGRINE FALCON			

QUAILS, PARTRIDGES & PHEASANTS

GREY PARTRIDGE			
RED-LEGGED PARTRIDGE			
COMMON PHEASANT			
GOLDEN PHEASANT			
COMMON QUAIL			

CRAKES & RAILS

WATER RAIL			
SPOTTED CRAKE			
LITTLE CRAKE			
BAILLON'S CRAKE			
CORNCRAKE			
COMMON MOORHEN			
COMMON COOT			
ALLEN'S GALLINULE			

CRANES

COMMON CRANE			

BUSTARDS

LITTLE BUSTARD			
MACQUEEN'S (HOUBARA) BUSTARD			
GREAT BUSTARD			

WADERS

EURASIAN OYSTERCATCHER			
BLACK-WINGED STILT			
PIED AVOCET			
STONE CURLEW			
CREAM-COLOURED COURSER			
COLLARED PRATINCOLE			
ORIENTAL PRATINCOLE			
BLACK-WINGED PRATINCOLE			
LITTLE (RINGED) PLOVER			
RINGED PLOVER			
KENTISH PLOVER			
GREATER SAND PLOVER			
EURASIAN DOTTEREL			
AMERICAN GOLDEN PLOVER			
PACIFIC GOLDEN PLOVER			
EUROPEAN GOLDEN PLOVER			
GREY PLOVER			
SOCIABLE PLOVER (SOCIABLE LAPWING)			
NORTHERN LAPWING			
RED KNOT			
SANDERLING			
SEMIPALMATED SANDPIPER			
LITTLE STINT			
TEMMINCK'S STINT			
WHITE-RUMPED SANDPIPER			
BAIRD'S SANDPIPER			
PECTORAL SANDPIPER			
SHARP-TAILED SANDPIPER			
CURLEW SANDPIPER			
PURPLE SANDPIPER			
DUNLIN			
BROAD-BILLED SANDPIPER			
STILT SANDPIPER			
BUFF-BREASTED SANDPIPER			
RUFF			

JACK SNIPE
COMMON SNIPE
GREAT SNIPE
LONG-BILLED DOWITCHER
EURASIAN WOODCOCK
BLACK-TAILED GODWIT
BAR-TAILED GODWIT
WHIMBREL
EURASIAN CURLEW
ESKIMO CURLEW
UPLAND SANDPIPER
SPOTTED REDSHANK
COMMON REDSHANK
MARSH SANDPIPER
COMMON GREENSHANK
GREATER YELLOWLEGS
LESSER YELLOWLEGS
GREEN SANDPIPER
WOOD SANDPIPER
TEREK SANDPIPER
COMMON SANDPIPER
SPOTTED SANDPIPER
RUDDY TURNSTONE
WILSON'S PHALAROPE
RED-NECKED PHALAROPE
GREY PHALAROPE

SKUAS
POMARINE SKUA
ARCTIC SKUA
LONG-TAILED SKUA
GREAT SKUA

GULLS
MEDITERRANEAN GULL
LAUGHING GULL
FRANKLIN'S GULL
LITTLE GULL
SABINE'S GULL
BLACK-HEADED GULL
SLENDER-BILLED GULL
RING-BILLED GULL
MEW (COMMON) GULL
LESSER BLACK-BACKED GULL
HERRING GULL, inc. YELLOW-LEGGED & CASPIAN GULL
ICELAND GULL
GLAUCOUS GULL
GREAT BLACK-BACKED GULL
BLACK-LEGGED KITTIWAKE
IVORY GULL

TERNS
GULL-BILLED TERN
CASPIAN TERN
LESSER CRESTED TERN
SANDWICH TERN
ROSEATE TERN
COMMON TERN
ARCTIC TERN
SOOTY TERN
LITTLE TERN
WHISKERED TERN
BLACK TERN
WHITE-WINGED BLACK TERN

AUKS
COMMON GUILLEMOT
RAZORBILL
BLACK GUILLEMOT
LITTLE AUK
ATLANTIC PUFFIN

SANDGROUSE
PALLAS'S SANDGROUSE

DOVES & PIGEONS
FERAL PIGEON
STOCK PIGEON (DOVE)
COMMON WOOD PIGEON
EURASIAN COLLARED DOVE
EUROPEAN TURTLE DOVE

PARAKEETS
ROSE-RINGED PARAKEET

CUCKOOS
COMMON CUCKOO
YELLOW-BILLED CUCKOO
GREAT SPOTTED CUCKOO

OWLS
BARN OWL
LITTLE OWL
SCOPS OWL
SNOWY OWL
TAWNY OWL
LONG-EARED OWL
SHORT-EARED OWL
TENGMALM'S OWL

NIGHTJARS
NIGHTJAR

SWIFTS
SWIFT
PALLID SWIFT
PACIFIC SWIFT
ALPINE SWIFT

KINGFISHERS
COMMON KINGFISHER

BEE EATERS & THEIR ALLIES
EUROPEAN BEEEATER
EUROPEAN ROLLER
HOOPOE

WOODPECKERS
EURASIAN WRYNECK
GREEN WOODPECKER
GREAT SPOTTED WOODPECKER
LESSER SPOTTED WOODPECKER

LARKS
GREATER SHORT-TOED LARK
WOOD LARK
SKY LARK
CRESTED LARK
HORNED (SHORE) LARK

SWALLOWS & MARTINS
SAND MARTIN
BARN SWALLOW
RED-RUMPED SWALLOW
HOUSE MARTIN

PIPITS
RICHARD'S PIPIT
BLYTH'S PIPIT

TAWNY PIPIT
OLIVE-BACKED PIPIT
TREE PIPIT
PECHORA PIPIT
MEADOW PIPIT
RED-THROATED PIPIT
ROCK PIPIT
WATER PIPIT

WAGTAILS
YELLOW WAGTAIL, inc. BLUE, GREY-HEADED
CITRINE WAGTAIL
GREY WAGTAIL
PIED WAGTAIL, INCL WHITE WAGTAIL

WAXWINGS
BOHEMIAN WAXWING

DIPPERS
WHITE-THROATED DIPPER, inc BLACK-BELLIED

WRENS
WINTER WREN

ACCENTORS
HEDGE ACCENTOR (DUNNOCK)
ALPINE ACCENTOR

ROBINS
EUROPEAN ROBIN

NIGHTINGALES & THEIR ALLIES
THRUSH NIGHTINGALE
COMMON NIGHTINGALE
BLUETHROAT
RED-FLANKED BLUETAIL
SIBERIAN BLUE ROBIN

REDSTARTS
BLACK REDSTART
COMMON REDSTART

CHATS
WHINCHAT
STONECHAT

WHEATEARS
NORTHERN WHEATEAR
ISABELLINE WHEATEAR
PIED WHEATEAR
DESERT WHEATEAR
WHITE-TAILED (WHITE-CROWNED BLACK) WHEATEAR

THRUSHES
WHITE'S THRUSH
RING OUZEL
COMMON BLACKBIRD
FIELDFARE
SONG THRUSH
REDWING
MISTLE THRUSH
AMERICAN ROBIN

WARBLERS
CETTI'S WARBLER
LANCEOLATED WARBLER
COMMON GRASSHOPPER WARBLER
RIVER WARBLER
SAVI'S WARBLER
AQUATIC WARBLER
SEDGE WARBLER
PADDYFIELD WARBLER
BLYTH'S REED WARBLER

MARSH WARBLER
EURASIAN REED WARBLER
GREAT REED WARBLER
EASTERN OLIVACEOUS WARBLER
BOOTED WARBLER
ICTERINE WARBLER
MELODIOUS WARBLER
DARTFORD WARBLER
MARMORAS WARBLER
SPECTACLED WARBLER
SUBALPINE WARBLER
BARRED WARBLER
SARDINIAN WARBLER
LESSER WHITETHROAT
COMMON WHITETHROAT
GARDEN WARBLER
BLACKCAP
GREENISH WARBLER
ARCTIC WARBLER
PALLAS' LEAF WARBLER
YELLOW-BROWED WARBLER
HUME'S (YELLOW-BROWED) WARBLER
RADDE'S WARBLER
DUSKY WARBLER
WESTERN BONELLI'S WARBLER
WOOD WARBLER
COMMON CHIFFCHAFF
WILLOW WARBLER

CRESTS
GOLDCREST
FIRECREST

FLYCATCHERS
SPOTTED FLYCATCHER
RED-BREASTED FLYCATCHER
COLLARED FLYCATCHER
PIED FLYCATCHER

BEARDED TIT (PARROTBILLS)
BEARDED TIT

TITS
LONG-TAILED TIT
MARSH TIT
WILLOW TIT
CRESTED TIT
COAL TIT
BLUE TIT
GREAT TIT

NUTHATCHES
WOOD NUTHATCH

TREECREEPERS
EURASIAN TREECREEPER

PENDULINE TITS
EURASIAN PENDULINE TIT

ORIOLES
EURASIAN GOLDEN ORIOLE

SHRIKES
ISABELLINE SHRIKE
RED-BACKED SHRIKE
LESSER GREY SHRIKE
GREAT (NORTHERN) GREY SHRIKE
SOUTHERN GREY SHRIKE
WOODCHAT SHRIKE

CORVIDS
EURASIAN JAY
BLACK-BILLED MAGPIE
SPOTTED NUTCRACKER
RED-BILLED CHOUGH
EURASIAN JACKDAW
ROOK
CARRION CROW
HOODED CROW
COMMON RAVEN

STARLINGS
COMMON STARLING
ROSY STARLING

SPARROWS
HOUSE SPARROW
EURASIAN TREE SPARROW

VIREOS
RED-EYED VIREO

FINCHES & CROSSBILLS
CHAFFINCH
BRAMBLING
EUROPEAN SERIN
EUROPEAN GREENFINCH
EUROPEAN GOLDFINCH
EURASIAN SISKIN
COMMON LINNET
TWITE
LESSER REDPOLL
COMMON REDPOLL ['MEALY' REDPOLL]
ARCTIC REDPOLL
TWO-BARRED CROSSBILL
COMMON CROSSBILL
PARROT CROSSBILL
TRUMPETER FINCH
COMMON (SCARLET) ROSEFINCH
COMMON BULLFINCH
HAWFINCH

AMERICAN SPARROWS
LARK SPARROW
WHITE-THROATED SPARROW

BUNTINGS
LAPLAND LONGSPUR (BUNTING)
SNOW BUNTING
YELLOWHAMMER
PINE BUNTING
CIRL BUNTING
BLACK-HEADED BUNTING
YELLOW-BREASTED BUNTING
ORTOLAN BUNTING
RUSTIC BUNTING
LITTLE BUNTING
REED BUNTING
CORN BUNTING